MICHEL QUOIST

Christ is
Alive!

Translated by J.F. Bernard

GILL AND MACMILLAN

Published in Ireland by
Gill and Macmillan Ltd
Goldenbridge
Dublin 8
with associated companies throughout the world
© Michel Quoist, 1970
Translation © 1971 Doubleday & Co., Inc.
0 7171 0507 5

Printed in China

Printing history
10   9   8   7

THE CARDINAL ARCHBISHOP OF PARIS

November 20, 1969
32, rue Barbet de Jouy
Paris VII

Dear Father Quoist,

Light must not be hidden under a bushel basket; it must be used to light our way. To that effect, you preach Jesus Christ the Saviour ardently and effectively, and these pages are indeed the Good News. May they be read by everyone who is uncertain and trying to find his way.

Your words also bear witness to your faith. We priests and bishops, pastors of the faithful gathered together within the Church, have been made responsible for the Word; and the preaching of the Gospel today requires both courage and experience.

I am delighted to have the opportunity once more to express my gratitude for your apostolic work and to assure you of my continuing friendship.

+ François Cardinal Marty
Archbishop of Paris

Contents

classified as 'popularisations'—are read only by priests, religious, seminarians, and by a few cultivated (and more or less clericalised) laymen. We do not take into account how much of what we write passes over the heads, and even more 'over the lives', of most of the People of God. We do not put ourselves in the reader's place. We flit about in a world of ideas and notions which is alien to him. We use a specialised vocabulary which he finds incomprehensible. It has often happened that I've loaned a particularly good book—one which, moreover, sold very well—to authentic Christians who were, as well, very intelligent and cultivated. Usually, the book has been returned only partially read; or, if the reader persevered to the end, he did so without interest or profit and out of a sense of duty. Any priest who works with Christians interested in understanding their lives and their faith will tell you the same thing. If they try to draw up a list of religious books they can recommend to such Christians, they find the list reduced to a very few titles.

I often travel abroad, and when I do I suffer because I cannot make myself understood without an interpreter. I do not know the language of my audience; but I do not say, 'Let them learn French. I'll come back when they can understand me.' I say instead, 'I'll have to learn their language.' But then, since I don't have the time, I have recourse, regretfully, to an interpreter.

Similarly, when we preach Jesus Christ, when we want to help Christians deepen their faith, we make ourselves understood little or not at all. What we must do is learn the language of our contemporaries. We must not try to set up courses for them to learn ours. We must attempt to enter into their way of thinking, into their mentality; we must not try to coax them out of their universe and into ours. We do not demean ourselves in all this, and we do not compromise the spiritual wealth that we wish to communicate. I wonder why we are always inclined to confuse the *form* in which those riches have been transmitted with the *content*, the message that they contain.

In writing this book—as with my earlier books—I have consulted not only with theologians, but also with its readers-to-be. There is not a page that has not been read and reread by several of the latter, both young and old, taken from various walks of life. I carefully noted the terms, the explanations, the words which they found confusing or unclear, and, without sacrificing the substance or even subtracting from what I had intended to say, I have retranslated such terms, explanations, and words. Some people say that to translate is to betray. I agree—if the translator is not perfectly the master of the language into which he is translating. And it is for that reason that I have asked the help of those who could correct what I had written. The result is certainly not a study in perfection; but it is an effort. (I thought I should mention this, because it is an effort that I must pursue further.)

Some readers will be surprised at the absence of 'technical terms' in this work. And, in fact, I have been at pains to avoid such terms. This is a somewhat dangerous procedure. Theologians make use of a vocabulary in which words have a precise meaning, and it is much easier to make use of that vocabulary than to try to express oneself in the words of everyday life. Nonetheless, our contemporaries—and the young, particularly—no longer understand the words and expressions of the theologians. That may be unfortunate, but it is a fact. I have therefore tried to avoid all technical terminology.

There are those who measure the 'depth' of a book in terms of its obscurity. 'What a wealth of thought!' they exclaim, when they have to read a chapter three times in order to understand it. Such confused and pedantic spirits notwithstanding, I have tried at all times to be as clear as possible. I am sorry if, because of that, I am branded as 'superficial'. It is not easy to be simple. If anyone reads parts of this book more than once, I hope it will be to meditate on them and not because they are obscure and difficult to understand.

I must end this preface with an appeal to theologians and to laymen jointly. It is necessary that there be men who study problems scientifically; and it is necessary that there be men who translate these findings into a language intelligible to our contemporaries. I don't believe that the same man can take on both jobs at the same time; he would risk neglecting one or the other task—and would probably end up by doing neither of them very well.

We need the *work* of the theologians. There are vital questions before today's Christians, and who will help us to resolve them if there are no specialists hard at work? But the specialists, for their part, should resist the temptation to speak too often, to write too hurriedly. Let them work in silence; and let them give us, from time to time, the benefit of their learning. But let them leave to the 'translators' the task of communicating such fruits to the People of God.

The best translators are those who work at translating a foreign language into their mother tongue. Therefore, the best 'translators' of doctrine for men of our time will be laymen. Only laymen are fully involved in life. Let them acquaint themselves with the work of the great theologians; and let them translate it for their brothers. But let them also live Jesus Christ today and bear witness to him for us. Why must almost all works of spirituality be written by priests and religious? Let the layman take up the pen—not to criticise (which is what some would make the layman's function), but to preach Christ Jesus.[1] The absence of the layman's voice in the Church is becoming more and more painfully clear.

'You are too optimistic,' some readers will tell me. I won't defend myself against that charge. On the contrary, I'll thank those readers, for I regard such an accusation as a compliment. Sometimes I am tempted to be pessimistic; but if I give in to the temptation, I feel guilty about it.

I am indeed optimistic about the world today. Too optimistic? I don't think so. We are never too optimistic when we believe in the Risen Christ living his mystery at the very heart of the world. I think the gravest sin of Christians today is fear. Evil, sin, death—we must keep those things in mind, of course; but beyond them, and in the same glance, we must see Christ victorious. Many people say, 'Everything is falling apart. A world is passing away.' But I say, 'A world is being born.' Death exists, but Jesus Christ has conquered death. Christ is alive!

[1] We have made a step in this direction by establishing a series called *Visages du Christ* (Faces of Christ), which is being published by Les Éditions Ouvrières, Paris. The series consists of authentic journals, letters, texts, etc. written by modern Christians who had no intention of publishing their manuscripts. We hope in this way to make available to modern man a true picture of contemporary Christian life. *Publisher's Note:* Paul Gallet's *Freedom to Starve*, Gill and Macmillan 1970, is the first of this series to be available in English translation.

PART I

PART 1

1. Are There Any New Christians?

Are we witnessing the birth of a new kind of Christianity? No doubt we are. Humanity is in the process of evolution, of mutation. Man's discoveries astonish even man. He has made himself master of atomic energy and, like every other conquest of a form of energy, this victory signals a veritable leap forward in man's domination over nature. Now electronic computers give man answers that it would otherwise take years, or a lifetime, to calculate. These machines, more efficient than the combined effort of thousands of human brains, control—and will control more and more as time goes on—the progress of man and the world. Man is beginning to explore the universe itself as a prelude to taking possession of it. His power over life is growing, and the time will come when, having reached its very source, he will be able to control it, protect it, and prolong it more and more.

In the final analysis man can truly be man only if he is aware of humanity, and this is even more the case today than it was yesterday. Men, wherever they may be, can no longer ignore other men. Everywhere, regardless of social class, nation, and race, men are growing; everywhere they are conscious of their human dignity; they are shaking off the chains of servitude; they are reaching up to, and demanding, total development. Nothing, no one, will be able to prevent this radical transformation of the world. The striving of the peoples of the world, their battles, the blood that they shed throughout the world for their freedom, is a tidal wave on the ocean of humanity; it is an immense and sorrowful sigh from a body which only yesterday had not been fully born but which today, in all its members, demands that it be allowed to live in the full light of day.

The man who lives, and will live, in this new world will have a life very different from that of his predecessors—even his immediate predecessors. And the Christian of today, who belongs to this mutating race of humans and who, with humanity, explores these new paths, will not be able to live his Christianity except within the framework of these new developments. The grace of Christ must inevitably lead him to a new form of contemplation, to new prayers, to new commitments; that is, to a new form of the Christian life. Today's Christian will not live as did yesterday's Christian. He cannot, and he does not wish to. He must not.

The Church, the People of God, is also going forward in time. Certainly, she has received from Jesus Christ, once and for all time, the inexhaustible treasury of Revelation. But the Church, on the one hand, must never cease exploring that treasury, in the diversity of its means, in order to be able to live in the today of her history; and, on the other hand, the Church, conscious of the requirements of human life at a particular moment in time, and studying that life in a spirit of love, must make it her task to shed light on whatever aspects of the Mystery of Christ are needed to enable men to live in their time. We are at the confluence of two worlds; we are at the dawn of a new age of humanity. And so, the Church, led by the Holy Spirit, felt the need to gather in Council in order to study her very nature so as to emerge renewed and cleansed of that human dross which has weighed her down, dimmed her glory, and stifled the Word. Then, looking upon the world, the Church has set about the chore of studying those existential relations with which the Christian, by his very nature, binds himself to her, so as to guide him on the road of history. For that history is the stuff of which is made the history of the Kingdom itself.

The Christian, however, has need of more than light to find his way. He needs a witness to travel with him and guide him. The Holy Spirit, who has raised up saints for every age, also raises up everyday saints; and these men are visible signs of Jesus' love for his people. It is their way of living Christ today that, little by little, initiates us into a 'spirituality for the men of our time'.

When we say that new 'witnesses' are needed for our time, it is not a matter of calling into question the value of the Christian life of yesterday. That life, that way of living Christ, was a sign for the contemporaries of our predecessors; but it cannot remain such for men of today. On the contrary. Certain attitudes and certain approaches, if they remain clothed in the forms of the past, will become 'counter-witnesses'.

Charity, for example, will always remain charity: 'Love one another as I have loved you.' But the road which leads from Jerusalem to Jericho has been extended to the ends of the earth, and our neighbours are now not only those who live in our vicinity, but also those of our social class, of our ethnic group, of our country, and of all the intermediate human groups to which we belong. Would the black man in America really be loving his neighbour if he contented himself with caring for the wounds of his brother and did not fight with all his strength for the liberation of all the brothers of his race? Would the labourer really be loving his neighbour if he were willing to lend an associate some money 'till payday', but did not join the battle for a living wage and social justice? To be sure, charity remains the same in its source, which is the infinite love of Jesus. But charity today must be lived differently from what it was yesterday. To old-fashioned charity a new dimension must be added: that by virtue of which man is reached through the intermediary of socialised structures.

(It would be easy to give other examples based on the way in which we must live other Christian virtues. We have but to reflect a little on poverty, obedience, and so forth.)

For today's Christians to be intelligible signs of love-charity to their contemporaries, they must, in the midst of the world, translate the eternal love of Jesus *into the actions of modern men*.

It is often said that modern man is a non-believer, that he rejects God. That may be. But too often the God that modern man rejects—the God that he believes to be the God of the Christians—is only a caricature. Somewhere, there has been a terrible misunderstanding. We have expressed ourselves very badly. We have lived badly. And so we have not made ourselves understood. We have spoken an unintelligible language in our churches and sacristies and meeting halls; and we did not have enough interpreters capable of translating into living language the eternal Word which is intended for every man. Jesus Christ came among us, and 'his own knew him not'— because we have too often exiled God from the company of man, from the very life that he came to participate in; because we have declared our love in a foreign language.

The Holy Spirit none the less continues to work in the heart of man and in the heart of humanity. He still prepares every man for the coming of the Saviour. He is present in the highest aspirations of men, of races and peoples today. And even if the latter, proud and impatient as rebellious adolescents who reject their fathers, reject, for the moment, both false gods and the living God—then let us have sense enough to realise (and patience and faith enough to believe) that man is experiencing merely a crisis of growth. It is a crisis that will resolve itself if only we are able, not to condemn, but to love.

It is true that, in a way, many men are in the process of conversion to a kind of natural religion, to the religion of man and his total development, of justice, peace, and happiness. But it is also true that man, God's creature, retains in himself a taste for the infinite. Man is insatiable. He knows his strength, and he wants to be ever stronger. He wants to master the universe. But when he has mastered the universe, he will still be unsatisfied. He will quickly see that his ambitions do not originate within himself; and he will realise that purely human accomplishments cannot satisfy those aspirations. Unconsciously, man senses and looks for a Strength, a Love: Someone. If we know how to proclaim and reveal Jesus Christ, then one day man will discover him—not at the end of the road of human achievement, but in the middle of it, within himself.

Modern man, who seems so far from God, in fact is not very far. Indeed, he has never been so close to the *true* God. In the midst of man's unbelief, faith awaits.

Let them take heart, those men of little faith who believe in the seed, but not in the ear of corn; who welcome the infant but reject the inevitable adolescent and then the adult. We must believe in the process of life. And when that life is that of Christ who beats a path to the heart of man and of the world, then to believe in life is a virtue— that of hope.

How excruciating is the fear of those 'well-disposed' Christians who mourn and lament the 'loss of faith'—of others. How deceptive is the good will of those who mobilise to defend the faith as though they were preparing to fly to the aid of a beaten and retreating army. Let them stop their trembling. Let them still their battle cries. Let them put away their weapons. Let them learn that their fear betrays a basic lack of faith. How can one believe in a Risen God who loses battles and who needs someone to defend him? How can one believe in a love which is unable to declare itself, a love which has become sterile and incapable of giving life? Christians should at least have faith! Let there be no more of this 'unbelief of the believers' that does so much harm. Jesus Christ has come. *He has saved the world.* He is risen. He does not stand there trembling, waiting for his disciples to defend him. He waits to be announced, to be revealed; and man, consciously or not, today more than ever, waits for the Good News. He is not going to meet Jesus Christ automatically, either at the end of or during his quest for human development. It is up to the new Christians to introduce Christ to him by joining in man's battles, progress, and aspirations.

But what are those aspirations which Christians, since they too are men of their time, also feel? We shall see that, far from being extraneous to Christianity, they are part and parcel of it.

2. Christianity and the Aspirations of Modern Man

The normal man of today wants above all to be fully a man. He wants to develop to the maximum degree that 'humanity' which is his. He knows that he has come far since his remote ancestors crouched in caves; and he knows that he will go even further.

Man today believes in man. He is proud of man. He is conscious of his greatness, of his power over himself, over his fellow men, over the world and the universe. He believes with all his strength in technology, in science, in the organisation of the terrestrial city, in the possibility of a happiness of which he will be the author. He wants this happiness for himself, of course; but he wants it also for all men without exception, for he knows that there are many kinds of men on the face of the earth and that they all have a right to develop themselves fully.

But can man believe both in man and in God? Can he believe both in heaven and in earth? Is the development of the human the same as the diminution of the divine? In attempting to build up and dominate the world, will man destroy heaven? God is a jealous God, we are told, and he requires that, to be united with him, man must renounce himself and the world. In that case, what meaning does the world have? Must man turn toward God and despise the world, or must he turn toward man and forget God? Or should he attempt a compromise (as many do) and sacrifice one to the other, each in his turn, and condemn himself to the dissatisfaction of neither living fully his humanity nor loving fully his God? Such, in fact, is the fate

of many Christians—those who live in a state of half joy
and half sadness because they are never able to reconcile
their desire to be both of the race of man and of Christ.
And this is one of the chief sources of scandal to non-
Christians, who, when they see so many Christians living
in a state of dissatisfaction, are unable to believe in a Love
that does not fulfil.

The Gospel tells us that if we want to follow Christ,
we must deny ourselves, die to ourselves. The Gospel says
that the kingdom of heaven is not of this world. And yet,
we love the excitement of life; we love beauty; and we
believe in a love which gives life. We love mankind; and
when humanity suffers, we suffer. We love the world, and
we take pride, as others do, when we see it becoming better.
And we want to take part, with all our strength, in that
process of amelioration.

How foolish we have been. We have allowed these
terrible—and utterly false—alternatives to become rooted
in the minds of many Christians. Today, we must show
them not only that they can be proud of being men, but also
that it is an obligation for them to *be* men as fully as
possible and to fight so that all of their brothers, all over
the world, may attain the highest degree of development
as human beings. We must show them that to take possession of the world, to dominate it, to use it and to love it, is
not to abandon God; rather, it is to obey God, to give
glory to God—and to bear in mind that one day God will
expect a full accounting of how we have managed the job.
Christians must be the most militant of those who strive
for human development; they must work harder than anyone else, by means of technology, science, and sweat, for
the conquest and control of nature. And they must not do
this as a more or less optional 'good work', as a means
of 'witnessing' before non-Christians, but because it is

their obligation as men and as children of God. Those who worry about a possible 'religion of man' shall see that it is Jesus Christ who is at the heart of that great work of creation; it is Jesus Christ who summons man to work with him; it is Jesus Christ who will lead mankind to the transcendental fulfilment that awaits it. To many, unfortunately, the very possibility of that fulfilment comes as a total surprise; and the fault is ours. But let us be patient with ourselves. If we are faithful to Christ, and faithful too to mankind and to the world, then Christ will be revealed.

Like that man who believes in man and in the reconstruction of the world, young people, in ever greater numbers, are asking questions about the meaning of life; and the answers of the adult world do not satisfy them. Their agony is expressed in an escape from the rigid life structures of that society which they reject, or in open revolt against institutions and persons. There is nothing surprising in that. A flower, if it were intelligent, would not be willing to live, to grow, to suffer, and to bloom for no one and no reason. It would certainly want to be beautiful; but it would want to be beautiful for someone.

This existential agony of the young is much less in evidence in underdeveloped countries and among the lowest social classes than in more affluent classes and nations. It seems that as soon as man is freed from the need to strive for the necessities of life, for a minimum of assured comfort, then he immediately begins to ask himself a basic question: What is the meaning of this life, and what is the reason for its limitations? Thus, unless we discover how to give a meaning to the life of men today—and especially to that of the young, who are less materialistic, more authentic, and more demanding—we can expect to see mankind torn apart by that terrible agony which follows the suspicion that life is, in effect, meaningless and absurd; that man is great, beautiful, and happy for, and with, no one—that is, with no one who is the inexhaustible source and purpose of happiness.

Indeed, it is obvious that the 'age of human agony' looms on the horizon of contemporary history; and already many young people have fallen victim to that plague. For someone to live as a man, he must know why he lives, what is the meaning of the moment of history in which he lives, what is the importance of each instant, each event, each encounter. Either the world is meaningless and therefore life is not worth living, or else the drama of life is being directed by a great Love, a great Idea. Today, Christianity can no longer be the caricature that some have made of it by reducing it to a complex of moral rules and religious rites—rules and rites which one can observe easily enough without their having one iota of influence upon one's personal or social life. Christianity today must be the beacon which lights up every human path; the Life which animates all life. Christianity must give a meaning to all of history, to the universe, to mankind, and also to each particle of matter and to each movement and instant of existence. Through Christ, modern man must be rescued from the temptation of the absurd.

Many men, however, are not ready to ask themselves questions about the basic meaning of the happiness they have attained through blood and sweat. The workers of the world are still fighting to live, and to live as men—that is, as responsible men. For that, in the final analysis, is what it is all about.

It is true that some workers, intimidated by statistics showing a supposedly regular rise in their buying power, hypnotised by the flicker of their television screens, lulled by the murmur of their washing machines, consider themselves to be relatively well off. These are the defeated; those who have abandoned, momentarily or permanently, the battle for total dignity for themselves and their fellow workers. It is also true, however, that the great masses of the people have, through the inspiration of a few men, come to realise that the earth belongs to all mankind. They know that each man, as a responsible individual, should have the means to accomplish the task that has been entrusted to him; that is, the conquest and building-up of the world by work. And he should be able to do this not in the role of a mere functionary, but as a responsible man, in cooperation with his brothers, through the interplay of just political, social, and economic structures. This movement of the masses will continue so long as the workers have not attained—beyond the bare necessities of life—the respect concomitant with that essential dignity.

Christians, generally, have been conspicuously absent from this mass movement of workers. One result of this absence has been that the workers have not discovered that the power of eternal Love, incarnated in Jesus Christ, could unite and mobilise them in the service of their brothers. Another has been that the workers have often become convinced that Christianity and the Church, the repositories of that infinite strength, are, in effect, a stronghold of inertia and an obstacle to progress—so much so that they must be destroyed before justice can triumph.

Certainly, the good works of some Christians have often been heroic; but those good works, though they have been a striking form of witness for some, for others have been a counter-witness to the extent that they have not been accompanied by participation in the battle for social justice. The Church, in fact (as many have noted), never 'lost' the working classes, for she was never really present among the workers—and she has been especially absent from the 'labour movement', which is essentially an expression of the ideal of life and dignity.

For several years now, some Christians (who were long misunderstood, and often attacked, by their brethren) have been living their worker's life, their battles, and their Christianity, in the unity of a unique Love. Such men are exceptions; and yet, they are true Christians. Tomorrow, perhaps, there will be enough such Christians among the poor and the exploited not merely to give a meaning to the labour movement (which has a meaning of itself), but to give *all* its meaning to it.

The worker 'proletariat' is no longer alone in the world. There is now a proletariat of peoples, comprising the millions of men who are virtually slaves—slaves, many of whom die of hunger every year. Perhaps the sociologists can work out statistical tables to tell us how many tens of millions of men have died, in the last few decades, in the concentration camps of underdevelopment. Maybe then those who advocate the violent suppression of every revolutionary movement, on the grounds that such movements risk 'bloodshed' will begin to have second thoughts. One may wonder whether lives sacrificed to maintain 'law and order' are less precious than those sacrificed in 'disorder'. Is violence always justified when it is used to put down revolutions, and always unjustified when it is used to make revolutions?

Such are the agonising questions that are being asked today, the world over, by many men of good will, and by many young people, who can no longer bear to see generation after generation of their brothers die for no reason at all. Sooner or later, these men will rise up in revolution, to free their people. The only question that remains is: What revolution will it be?

Today, Christianity must be the crucible of true revolution. Now that it is a matter of freeing entire nations, we must not attempt—as we did with respect to the labour movement—to excuse ourselves from participation. For the underdeveloped peoples of the world can wait no longer. They know now that they are suffering unjustly. They know why they are oppressed. And they want to free themselves. But how? They are searching for a concept of humanity and of life that will give meaning to their battle and will give them the courage to act.

In some countries, the choice is still open. I am thinking particularly of the Latin American countries, in which ninety-five per cent of the population are baptised Catholics, and where many good men, in every class of society and at every age level, have come face to face with a painful question: Should they turn to another 'mystique', to another 'faith', to accomplish that revolution which Christianity has not been able to achieve? These men know that they have no need to ask the Church for instructions on the techniques of liberation; but some of them still hope that they may find—that they will be helped to find—in the Church that strength of Love which they need in order to fight, suffer, and win.

We must restore to Christianity the irresistible power of revolution that our selfishness, our stupidity and our exaggerated prudence have stifled. Jesus Christ is condemned by our timidity. He dies every day, in millions of the members of his Body. 'I was hungry,' he says, 'and you did not feed me. I was naked, and you did not clothe me.' Many of us, he forgives, 'for they know not what they do.' But now, let us know what we do. The good works, heroic though they may be, by which we silence our conscience are but a drop in the ocean so far as what they accomplish; even worse, they are an offence to the basic dignity of man unless they are accompanied by the gift of ourselves in the all-out battle for the radical reform of our political, economic, and social structures.

Let us acknowledge that we cannot save our souls unless we save man's body. Jesus Christ came to save the *whole* man; and that is the final purpose of the real revolution—of the revolution that each of us much preach and that each of us, in his own way, must accomplish.

3. A Spirituality for Contemporary Christians

The situation touched on in the preceding chapter is clear enough. We are waiting to see whether the modern world is indeed 'allergic' to Christianity. One of two things will happen. First, man will come to understand not only that there is no conflict between his human aspirations and Christianity, but also that Christianity can give their true meaning to those aspirations; and then many men will open their minds and hearts to the revelation of Jesus Christ. Or, modern man will continue to believe that there is a contradiction between those two elements, and then, helpless but still generous and open, he will continue to search elsewhere for a reason to live and to fight.

If this is true of the man of good will who is earnestly trying to find his way, it is no less true of the faithful Christian. The Christian, as we have already said, is a man of his time; he has the same anxieties and the same ideals as other men. If Christianity does not give him the answers to the vital questions that he asks, then he will abandon Christianity—as one abandons an old suit that, though useful in its time, has now become useless and out of fashion.

What is needed today is for the Christian to encounter God *in his everyday life*. Jesus can no longer be a distant stranger, respected and feared—or even loved—but uninvolved in life. And the Christian can no longer be merely a servant whose daily chores are only a test of his loyalty and a testimonial to his unswerving faith. Man knows that he is only a creature, and a weak and vulnerable creature at that; but he knows too that he has been offered the opportunity to become a son of God and a collaborator in the Kingdom that is being founded. He knows that he must diminish so that God may increase—but more and more he realises that it is not a question of self-annihilation but of the pure exercise of a freedom which, by opening up man to infinite Love, assures his full development both in time and in eternity.

In his spiritual life, therefore—that is, in his progress toward God—the Christian wants to commit his whole being. It is not sufficient for him to give an intellectual allegiance to this or that point of doctrine; and even less is he satisfied by emotional consolations, the charms of a fertile imagination, or merely physical manifestations of his submission to God. If he is to move toward God through Christ Jesus, his Saviour, then he wishes to do so with all of himself, in every act of his daily life, in his work, his leisure, his relationships, his loves, his struggles and the struggles of his brothers. Every day of his life, today's Christian becomes aware that he is not alone; he is in a certain neighbourhood, in a certain factory, in a certain club or social class; he is aware, in other words, that he is a member of the human community. He is surrounded by a people on the move and in company with them; and that people wants to meet his God.

This heartfelt desire to find Christ in daily life is not a vision or an illusion. Jesus Christ, in effect, is waiting for man at the very heart of the world. And man today, more than his predecessors, longs—too often in darkness, unfortunately—for the Risen Christ who lives his Mystery in human history. He senses, confusedly, that he will meet Christ on the way, a Christ who is there for everyone and in everything. He senses the presence of the divine Lover who is indifferent to nothing that concerns man, of the silent Companion of his labours who mixes his redeeming blood with man's daily sweat and works with man to build a world which will be transformed by the Father through the elements of the infinite which exist at the very centre of the temporal order. Man can no longer bear to struggle each day if that struggle is to remain forever at the level of earth, if God is to be absent from it, if it is not to be with God that he and his brothers live, love, and die.

God is there, and man knows it. God is waiting to love man and to work with him. And the success of man's life depends on his finding God. Can God be found? He calls to man in the world; but the world itself is noisy, distracting, and seductive. Many men in the world are concerned only with amusing themselves while waiting for death; while others, unknowing but proud, are convinced that they will somehow be able to eternalise their earthly happiness. But the Christian—have we been able to persuade him that his instincts are not mistaken, that God is indeed present in man's life? Have we been able to show him how to find God and how to work with God?

Unfortunately, the spirituality that we have attempted to teach laymen is not that of laymen but of monks. It is a spirituality shot through with the mystical experiences of vowed religious, with their methods, with the spiritual exercises they have formulated. The most renowned saints, those who are recognised as founders of 'schools' of spirituality, those who are held up as examples, are almost always religious. Most often, they have attained sanctity by 'leaving the world'. And, of course, priests have all been educated in seminaries which were little more than monasteries; they have all spent many years living like monks (a life which they were unable to continue in the active ministry). They then attempted to pass on to the faithful what they had learned and lived in those monasteries; and to the most devout of the faithful they suggested entering a 'Third Order', in which the layman would find, rather than a spirit of sharing, the framework of monastic life adapted to persons living in the world. Certain lay spiritual movements—even those which call themselves 'action' movements—have been so influenced by this monastic orientation that they have tried to reproduce the monastic rule of life, with its charters, chapters, sessions of self-confession and self-abasement, and all the rest. But other action movements—that is, organisations aimed at the integration of faith and life—have, in the past few years, discovered the elements of an authentic 'layman's' spirituality. In the latter instance, however, only a few priests were able to be of use to the organisations concerned; and those few were the priests who were capable of grasping the fact that their function was not to *teach* the Christian life to laymen, but to learn life itself from them. And then those priests were able to be of service, to join with laymen in finding, not a doctrine, but a living Person.

Today, there are still religious who live in such a way as to let us know, somehow, that a man may be a contemplative in the midst of the world. But their testimony is no more directly applicable to laymen than was that of their predecessors. Such religious are present in the world, but they are not committed to the world. For the layman, however, it is in the midst of a commitment to the world that Jesus must be found and must be lived.

The faithful are told: 'God is in the desert. You must separate yourself from the world and enter into solitude if you want to find God. God is in silence; if you want to hear him, you must flee the noise of the world. Only through contemplation can you know God, and an active life destroys contemplation. Forget the preoccupations of the world, for they are obstacles to an encounter with God.'

But the layman lives in the midst of noise, surrounded by crowds, overwhelmed by necessary activities. He works in an office, surrounded by employees, and pores over columns of figures. He works in a factory, noise is everywhere, and he is the slave of a machine which becomes like a part of himself. He is packed into a bus, jammed into the underground. He is in a flat whose paper-thin walls bring him the sounds of the lives of his neighbours. He is in a kitchen, always a little behind in washing the clothes, preparing the vegetables, bathing the baby, getting the children off to school. He is at the beach, in a restaurant, in front of the television set. He is always busy, always worried —about the end-of-the-month bills, about the shoes he must buy, about getting the washing machine mended, about the expenses he must meet, about the stock market. He belongs to a family and to a social milieu; he lives in a particular community, in a city, in a nation. He belongs to a union and goes to innumerable meetings. He agitates, struggles, fights for various movements and groups. *He is a part of life.* And yet, we tell him that he must separate himself from life if he is to find God.

Perhaps there are several classes of Christians. The first would comprise a privileged class, the super-Christians, the aristocrats of the spiritual life, who are called to love Christ in solitude, far from the world, and to participate in a special relationship with him. The second class would be composed of a sort of spiritual *bourgeoisie* who, following the example of the aristocrats, are able to shut themselves up in their rooms (because each of them is able to afford a private room), attend retreats regularly and spend Holy Week in a monastery, read books of spirituality, and take courses in the Bible—because they have enough education to do so, or because they are unmarried, or because they can affort servants to care for their families—or because they have the time to do all these things since they refuse to become involved in social and political matters, in order to concentrate on 'what is essential'. And finally, in last place, there would be the great mass of the people, those who are condemned to live in the hurly-burly of the world, jostled, crushed, sacrificed; who are able from time to time, by a heroic act of the will, to tear themselves away and, despite a thousand worries and distractions, to catch a glimpse of Christ—just enough of a glimpse to leave a bitter aftertaste of dissatisfaction.

If God is truly present only 'in the desert' and in silence, then he is not accessible to the majority of men today. And in that case, if the purpose of the Incarnation was to join Christ to man in the whole of life, we may say that the Incarnation has been a fiasco.

Fortunately, that is not the case. We know—through the words of a certain number of Christians—that the Holy Spirit is in the process of teaching us anew today that, although the gifts and vocations of each man are different, every man is called to meet Jesus and to unite himself to Jesus within the framework of that human life to which Providence has assigned him. The Holy Spirit is telling us that life today—like life yesterday—is not a 'punishment'; it is a gift of love from the Creator. It is not an obstacle to divine union; it is the customary place for a meeting with Christ. Man is not condemned to live as 'an exile' in this 'valley of tears'; he is invited to participate, as a friend and a brother, in the mission entrusted to Jesus by the Father. It may be that participation has become burdensome and painful; if so, it is not by God's will but by man's sin, for its essential characteristic is the infinite joyfulness of the Resurrection.

We may be certain that, guided by the Holy Spirit, the

laity will give to the Church those new saints of which she has such need. And, in the meantime, we must, with our brother laymen, search, pray, and live the adventure of sanctity in new ways.

PART II

4. Jesus Christ and Faith

At the centre of history, at the centre of the world, and the centre of humanity, there is the Event, the unique Event: Jesus Christ, the Son of God, made man.

Jesus Christ appeared in history two thousand years ago, in a segment of space called Palestine, as a Man among men, as the Man-God. His mission was to reveal the infinite love of the Father—a love of which he himself is the sign. He is the sacrament *par excellence*, in which all other sacraments are included and from which they all emanate and take their power. He came to reveal the eternal plan of the Father's love, to reveal 'the message which was a mystery hidden for generations and centuries' (*Col.* 1:26); the plan by which all men are to become the Father's 'adopted sons, through Jesus Christ' (*Eph.* 1:5); 'the hidden plan he so kindly made in Christ from the beginning, to act upon when the times had run their course to the end: that he would bring everything together under Christ, as head, everything in the heavens and everything on earth' (*Eph.* 1:10). He came to gather together the scattered children of God into one people, one Church.

We know now that all things had been conceived in Christ from eternity, that all things are accomplished in him; and therefore we know that the Mystery of Jesus Christ permeates all things, affects all men—present, past, and future—pervades all of history and all of the universe both in time and beyond time into eternity. Jesus Christ is at the beginning, in the middle, and at the end. He is before, during, and after: 'I am the Alpha and the Omega, the

First and the Last, the Beginning and the End' (*Rev.* 22:13).
And the eternal plan of the Father's love is the total Mystery
of Christ.

Thus, nothing and no one is beyond that mystery of love.
No man, whoever he be, with faith or without it, can
escape from it. Every man is vitally affected. Since the
Event, man cannot have the same view of himself, of other
men, and of the world. He can no longer live, work, and
love in the same way, for the Event has given a meaning to
everything; it has given its own meaning—a total and final
meaning—to all of creation. And it has done this, not by
destroying what went before, but by perfecting and
accomplishing all things in itself.

This historic Event, the coming of Christ on earth, is
the sensible, visible, and efficacious sign of the total and
invisible Mystery of Jesus Christ. And the whole of our
Christian lives, all of our 'spirituality', is characterised by,
and receives its direction from, the degree to which we
understand the Event.

Either we meet the Son of God, as it were, in Jesus as
a historical personage, and we allow ourselves to be loved
by him and to imitate him in our lives. In that case we
bind ourselves to him by a personal relationship of friendship so that our lives are influenced only indirectly, from
without, and (probably) only in part, by Christ. Or, on
the other hand, we believe in and we live Jesus Christ in
his total Mystery—and then our lives are affected directly,
from within, and wholly, so that the years of our lives
become a prolonged effort to achieve *incorporation* into
Jesus. We offer him our lives so that through them—in
every instant of time and in every act and thought— Jesus
Christ may make present to us in time his eternal Mystery
by making us live, with him and in him within the framework of our day-to-day existence, in union with all of

mankind and with the world, the ineffable mystery of love which is the eternal plan of the Father.

It is to this sharing of himself that Christ invites us.

If, however, we are to understand that to which we are called, we must consider Christ in what we might call his 'dimensions'. And the first question that comes to mind, of course, is: Who is Jesus Christ?

We have already said that he is a historical personage, whose life (at least in its most important events) is known to us, and whose message we know essentially from Jesus' own words. He was a man, we know, who lived for about thirty-three years on earth, and whose memory is still vivid in human history. And we know that he was the Son of God. St John saw, listened to, and touched this God-made-man; and while he was still trembling with the excitement of this unbelievable encounter, he wrote: 'Something which has existed since the beginning, that we have heard, that we have seen with our own eyes; that we have watched and touched with our hands: the Word, who is life—this is our subject. That life was made visible: we saw it and we are giving our testimony, telling you of the eternal life which was with the Father and has been made visible to us. What we have seen and heard we are telling you so that you too may be in union with us, as we are in union with the Father and with his Son Jesus Christ. We are writing this to you to make our own joy complete' (1 *John* 1:1–4).

The Christ of which St John writes is the same Risen Christ who mysteriously lives among us today. Christ is his whole Body—that is to say, the entire universe, all the matter and all the life that would not exist if he did not sustain it by being present in it: 'He is the image of the unseen God and the first-born of all creation, for in him

were created all things in heaven and on earth: everything
visible and everything invisible . . . and he holds all things
in unity' (*Col.* 1:15–17). It was from matter and from
life that he took his flesh; 'and the Word was made flesh'
—flesh that the Father raised up and took to himself for
eternity. And therefore matter and life should be wholly
contained in him: 'He has let us know the mystery of his
purpose . . . that he would bring everything together under
Christ, as head, everything in the heavens and everything
on earth' (*Eph.* 1:9–11).

Of this Body of Christ, therefore, we are all members
—including, in a very special and privileged way, the
poorest of our brothers and even those who seem to be the
farthest from Christ: 'I was in prison and you came to see
me' (*Matt.* 25:36)—or 'you did not come to see me.' And
therefore it is the human race in its entirety which grows
each day, and will continue to grow until the end of time
when Christ's Body will have become 'fully mature' (*Eph.*
4:13).

This Body of Christ is the Kingdom of God; it is the
City of God; it is the Church, that enormous complex
within which human beings and the Holy Spirit work
together: 'So you are no longer aliens or foreign visitors:
you are citizens like all the saints and part of God's house-
hold. You are part of a building that has the apostles and
prophets for its foundations, and Christ Jesus himself for
its main cornerstone. As every structure is aligned on him,
all grow into one holy temple in the Lord; and you too,
in him, are being built into a house where God lives, in
the Spirit' (*Eph.* 2:19–22).

Jesus' question is still valid: 'And you, who do you say
I am?' It is directed to each of us personally; and the
answer we give is a measure of the depth and dimension
of our faith.

The question which inevitably follows that of 'Who is Jesus Christ' is this: 'What is Christian faith?' Christian faith, obviously, is not merely a felt emotion; nor a purely intellectual conviction; nor adherence to a moral or religious code; nor even a 'belief in a creator-God (which would be deism; and how many self-styled Christians, unfortunately, are no more than deists).

Christian faith is, first of all, an encounter with God by means of the grace of the Father. It is Love, brought to mankind by the Son of God. It is also an act of trust made in Christ Jesus as a living person, as someone in the truth of whose words and life we can believe. And finally, it is a commitment within the Church, the People of God, as an institution which lives in time the Mystery of Christ. That is, it is a free and conscious participation, within Love, in the mission of Christ on earth: the realisation of the plan of the Father. 'If anyone wishes to be my disciple'—that is, to be a Christian—'let him follow me.'

Thus, in the final analysis, the 'mature' Christian is a man who (progressively) has encountered Christ as a historic personage; who has recognised him as the Son of God; who has made an act of trust in him; and who is bound to Jesus by a personal relationship of love which culminates in a basic identification and union with him. It is, furthermore—and necessarily—the man who finds Jesus Christ in his 'mystical dimension,' in his total Mystery, in order to live with him and in him. This Mystery is one which we must live as a people, as a Church, at a particular moment in time; in our life as a whole and in every instant and event of our life; occupying a certain space in the cosmos; within the geographical and sociological circumstances within which we find ourselves; and, finally, in the company of our brothers—that is, in all of the natural communities and societies within which we spend our lives.

Faith at that level may be classified as 'mature'. Why? Because it is the adolescent whose proper function it is to become aware of himself as a person, as someone distinct from his parents, as an autonomous being capable of entering into personal relationships with other autonomous beings. The adolescent, after a long exploration of himself (which leads, hopefully, to an understanding of himself), becomes more and more capable of friendship; he serves, as it were, an apprenticeship in human relations. At the same time, as a Christian, he becomes aware of his God in Jesus Christ, in a preliminary stage, as a friend, a model, and a leader.

On the road to maturity, the adolescent discovers subsequently that he is a person who lives in a society, in a world. Or else, he fails to adapt himself to his environment and therefore remains at the preceding stage of psychological development; that is, he lives as a stranger in the world, capable only of transitory and limited relationships, requiring direction and rules in order to keep him in line. The adolescent who is maturing properly, on the other hand, learns to integrate himself into the world and to take his place among his peers, to work out the problems implicit in personal confrontations and in common undertakings.

Similarly, the adult Christian must also go beyond a personal meeting with Jesus of Nazareth. Taking cognisance of the fact that he belongs to 'a people', to a Church situated in time and space, he must live, in the company of his brothers, all the dimensions of the Mystery of Jesus Christ. He must commit himself voluntarily not only to the observance of a law clearly and simply enunciated, but also to participation in a common work by determining, step by step, in every phase of his daily life, what is God's will both for himself and for the human race of which he is a member.

There are, no doubt, sincere and generous Christians today who are upset by the appearance of certain Christian life-styles, by attempts to resolve, in the light of faith, the novel problems of a changing world, by the efforts of some Christians to live in brotherhood with non-Christians. Those who are disturbed by such things seem to be basically maladjusted and immature in their faith. They are taking refuge in the security of the past, where, they hope, they will find doctrinal 'security', clear rules, predigested rituals, etc. They need the help of theologians, certainly; but, even more, such Christians need the help of psychology and psychiatry to help them travel the road toward maturity.

The world today has need of mature men. And it has equal need of mature faith.

The Mystery of Jesus Christ is unique. It is the eternal plan of the Father's love, which was lived historically by Christ in ancient Palestine and which is 'mysteriously' unfolded in and by the Risen Christ throughout time and history. We who contemplate that Mystery will never adequately grasp 'the breadth and the length, the height and the depth, until, knowing the love of Christ, which is beyond all knowledge, you are filled with the utter fullness of God' (*Eph.* 3:18–19). We must therefore—without losing sight, however, of the Mystery as a whole and of its unity—reflect successively on the Creation, the Incarnation, the Redemption, and the Resurrection. Those are all different aspects of the same love as lived by Christ on earth two thousand years ago, and lived now with him and in him by the whole Church, and, within the Church, by each individual Christian—and even, at another level, by all men.

The imperfection of our sight requires that we study individually each aspect of that unique Mystery of Jesus; but we must then contemplate them as a whole, each one in and with all the other aspects. Only in that way can the symphonic harmony of the Mystery be audible in all of its truth, as each part loses itself in the beauty of the whole.

What holds true with respect to meditation on the Mystery of Jesus is even more true when it is a question of living that Mystery. For there are such things as false virtues and false spiritualities which, in concentrating on only one aspect of the Christian life to the exclusion of all else, mutilate that life almost beyond repair. Thus, it would be a serious mistake to attempt to live the mystery of the Creation while ignoring that of the Incarnation, which lies at the very centre of the Creation. (And isn't that really the great temptation of the modern world? I mean, to accept and develop man and the world, but to ignore, at every step along the way, the necessity for the virtue of Love-Charity?)

The Incarnation itself cannot be lived authentically if it is not tied to the Redemption. Sin is always with us, and the grace of salvation cannot reach mankind unless, in the footsteps of Christ, man is able to do battle against evil and unless he is able to die to himself.

And finally, the Redemption cannot be lived without the Resurrection; for in Christ Jesus, beyond all suffering and all death, there is the infinite life and joy of Easter.

5. The Mystery of Creation

Creation is not yet finished. Not all the seed has been sown; not all the trees planted; not all the crops harvested. Not all the animals have been born; and man has not yet domesticated them all. And not all the factories have been built, nor all the bridges constructed, nor all the dams erected. There are still houses and cities to be built, satellites to be put into orbit, planets to be conquered. The creation of the universe, of life and matter, is still taking place in time, is being transformed by man, is not yet complete.

Mankind itself is developing. We, who have the obligation to work for our full development, are still creating ourselves. Such is the work of education—both the education which we receive and that which we give to ourselves as we grow in maturity; it is, in essence, a long process of balancing, harmonising, unifying, and developing all of our physical, intellectual, and spiritual energies by humanising and personalising them. It is also all of the instruction that we have received, the cultural acquisitions that we have made to enrich ourselves at the intellectual, artistic, and professional levels. And, finally, it is the interplay of our personal relationships within the framework of the natural societies within which we live; relationships which must deepen to the point of 'communion' and broaden to the extent that our human nature allows.

Every day, in living and still more in determining the course of his life, man is creating himself. And mankind, collectively, also continues its prodigious expansion. Man,

in the process of transforming himself by means of the
successive victories of past generations and of his own
efforts to rise still higher, is becoming greater and more
powerful with every passing century. He is also multiply-
ing himself rapidly—so much so that the rising birth rate
presents new problems to man's intelligence and to his
conscience. And finally, the 'body' of mankind is taking on
definition as it develops. Increasingly structured human
societies are being formed or strengthened and are establishing closer and closer bonds with other societies the
world over. Thus, we are far from the concept of a God
who, in one unique and definitive act, created the universe.
And creation, as a gesture of love on the part of the Father
and of the Son, continues in time.

Creation, therefore, is an integral part of the Mystery of
Christ. Nothing escapes the impact of the Event. It is in
Christ that creation begins, develops, and flourishes: 'He
is the image of the unseen God and the first-born of all
creation, for in him were created all things in heaven and
on earth: everything visible and everything invisible. . . .
Before anything was created, he existed, and he holds all
things in unity' (*Col.* 1:15–17); 'It is in him that we live
and move, and exist' (*Acts* 17:28); 'Through him all things
came to be, not one thing had its being but through him'
(*John* 1:3).

Thus, the Risen Christ is present throughout the prodigious development of mankind and the universe. He is the
centre of it and the Mover. Nothing of matter, of life, can
be created, transformed, or brought to its final form
without the all-powerful action of Jesus Christ. Creation
was conceived 'in him' from all eternity; and it is 'in him'
that it is being realised.

But if creation is the work of Christ, at every moment
both within us and around us, it is also the work of man.

God has so willed it from the very beginning, and he has entrusted the universe to man: 'God said, "Let us make man in our own image, in the likeness of ourselves"'—that is, man would share, among other things, God's role as creator—'"and let them be masters of the fish of the sea, the birds of heaven, the cattle, all the wild beasts and all the reptiles that crawl upon the earth"' (*Gen.* 1:26). And to mankind he also entrusted man: 'God created man in the image of himself, in the image of God he created them, male and female he created them. God blessed them, saying to them, "Be fruitful, multiply, fill the earth and conquer it"' (*Gen.* 1:27–28).

Man undertook his task—that of turning his individual and collective energies to the conquest of the earth and the universe by both knowledge and action, by bending it to his will, transforming and developing it for his own benefit and for the glory of God—but he undertook it slowly and painfully. For the undertaking includes in itself all of man's labours in science, technology, art, and all that he has accomplished through the labour of his hands and the effort of his reason.

At the same time, man himself has taken charge of the progress of mankind; of man's personal ascent toward the expanded horizons of knowledge, of conscience, and of freedom, by means of instruction and education; of the development of mankind by procreation, with love, within the family unit.

Man's responsibilities are exhilarating and exalting. Man begins with the gift of life and of his abilities; but, from that point, he decides and creates what he is to be. He decides to change the course of a river, to build a city, to explore the heavens, or to create a child. God, for his part, confirms, guides, and strengthens; but to man he leaves complete freedom of decision and of action. How far will he allow man to go in the exercise of his power of procreation? To what point will he allow man's power over matter and life to continue to grow? The modern world gives us some exciting indications of the answer— and some rather frightening indications too. What is certain, however, is that God, the infinitely loving Father, must be pleased to see his children develop themselves personally and accept the enormous responsibilities he has placed upon their shoulders. As at the beginning of time, when God invested man with dominion over the world, he continues to look upon his work and to see that it is very good indeed.

What, then, can we possibly fear?

Nothing. For the Christian least of all should be afraid of man's power over himself and the universe. On the contrary, he should be proud of it. We should never have left it to the Marxists to preach the nobility of labour, for we go much further than they in believing in it. For us, the world that we must build and the human race that we must glorify are all part of a divine Mystery. It is 'in Christ' that man and the universe have been created; but, just as they have not been created at one instant and for all time in one definitive act, so too it is in Christ that all men live and grow and that the universe develops and is brought under control. Thus, God, through the Son, has arranged an encounter of love at the very centre of labour, of every educational undertaking, and of human love. The creature is to encounter the Creator. Man's will is to become one with the divine will, and man's action is to be joined to the divine action. And the two, radically united, are to complete the work of creation.

But man can choose to be absent from that encounter. Some men refuse to recognise God and to unite themselves to him. They want to work alone, and they reject God either directly (by saying, in effect, 'mind your own business') or indirectly, by refusing to work in justice and for justice and dignity with their brother men. This is the eternal temptation for man: to make himself a god without God. 'You will be like gods,' says Satan. And so, man tries to build for himself 'a town and a tower with its top reaching heaven' (*Gen.* 2:4). Such is the folly of man, who becomes man-creator only in and with Christ Jesus: 'If Yahweh does not build the house, in vain the masons toil' (*Ps.* 127:1). Neither the philosophical materialism of Marxism nor the practical materialism of capitalism, therefore, is capable of preparing us for a glorious tomorrow. It is all up to the mature Christian, who must live the mystery of the Creation without forgetting the mystery of the Incarnation—who must live, in fact, the entire Mystery of Jesus.

There are many who are incapable of discerning the presence of God in the continuing work of creation. These are the truly underdeveloped. Because of insufficient information, or inadequate education, or simply because they have been overwhelmed by the mere struggle for existence, they are not in a position to believe in the presence of the infinite love of Jesus Christ which, in spite of sin (and it is indeed a question of sin), waits for them in order to perfect and redeem that creation by participating in it. But this is yet another aspect of the Mystery of Christ; that is, the mystery of the Redemption, which we will discuss later on.

Finally, we may say that many men simply do not know that Jesus Christ is waiting for them in the midst of all their efforts to develop man and the world by means of instruction, education and sweat. They do not know, because no one has bothered to tell them. Christians, who should have told them, were too often of the opinion that the development of mankind and of the universe was none of God's business—or at least that he was not directly concerned with it.

Such are the various drawing boards of creation, which are the predestined meeting places of Creator and creature. We tell Christians today that human love, divinised by the sacrament of marriage, is capable of leading one to Christ and uniting one to him. There are not two different times, for example, in conjugal love—that is, a time to live one's love, and a time to offer that love to God. There is only one time; and it is in the act of loving itself that we will love Jesus Christ. Not in 'offering up' an already existing human love.

We also tell Christians today that in all the acts of one's married life, even in the physical act of love, a man and wife live their love authentically and communicate God to one another.

To be sure, we should rejoice that the spiritual value of married life has finally been recognised. Even so, we must recognise that that concept is only one stage, one aspect, of a greater spirituality, a spirituality which affects all phases and the whole of one's life, a spirituality which modern man must discover in order to nourish himself from it. Otherwise, he condemns himself to a continued compartmentalisation of his life—to a divorce between his life and his Christian faith.

We have not preached enough to our fellow Christians the fact that, in their efforts to better themselves both individually and collectively, in their work, they can and must unite themselves to Jesus Christ. There is no sacrament, obviously, which divinises those aspects of human life; nevertheless, they are an integral part of the mystery of Creation, one of the facets of the total Mystery of Jesus

Christ, which is itself signified by, included in, and accomplished by that Sacrament of sacraments, the Eucharist.

Man, we have said, is not finished. He is still in the state of becoming, both individually and collectively; and he is creating himself—or not creating himself—by the act of living. In struggling to humanise and personalise himself, in struggling for his complete development—a development which he creates himself—man meets Jesus Christ. He meets Jesus Christ at every moment, at every turn. For Christ, in effect, has been at work since the beginning of creation in order to engender the sons whom the Father has wanted from all eternity.

We must therefore rid ourselves of that concept of man which tells us that man is simply man, once and for all; that man is fixed and complete in his being, a creature whose behaviour is liable to judgement according to a fixed hierarchy of values and according to whether or not one is a man-man or a Christian-man. We must no longer think of man as a being who subsequently will become 'a virtuous man' or a saint merely because he observes this or that special system of laws for Christian-man. For a Christian is not a person who lives in a special way. A Christian is a man who lives as a man and is continually becoming more of a man. It is as simple as that. It is by becoming a 'whole man'[1] that he will bear witness, for then he will represent to his brothers the perfect realisation of

---

[1] By a 'whole man' I mean one who is wholly open to divinisation in Jesus Christ. We will return to this subject when we discuss the mystery of the Incarnation. Suffice it to say here that God, from all eternity, has willed and loved not several kinds of men, but one kind; and the 'whole man', man fully developed and fully himself, is properly 'Man, the Son of God'.

that which God has intended for man from the beginning of time.

Christ came on earth to show us what a Perfect Man is. And he came to show us how to become perfect men. The hierarchical Church, when she counsels man, when she warns him, intends always to defend him and to defend his true development as a man. It is never her intention to diminish his humanity. Like Christ, the Church wants man to succeed. So far the Church. There are, however, individuals within that Church—churchmen, to be exact— who, as incompetent teachers, have made 'virtuous Christians', 'devout laymen', and even 'holy priests and religious' out of individuals who were, in fact, nothing more than sick and unbalanced men and women; and such 'spiritual formation' is nothing more than monstrous deformation. Certainly, we do not mean to call into question the sincerity and generosity of these poor souls whose efforts were offered to—and no doubt received by— God. They deceived themselves, no doubt; but only because they themselves were deceived. Still, we have no right to present to the Father men who are unbalanced, or deformed—monstrosities, in other words. Except in the case of a 'miracle', God leaves it to doctors to cure the sick. Grace does not cure a disordered mind; that is up to the psychotherapists and the psychologists. (But here again, let us recall that the doctor, the psychotherapist, and the psychologist, in their work of healing, collaborate with Christ to bring man to his proper development.)

Some of the Christians in certain organisations and 'societies' and 'confraternities' and 'movements' have attempted to escape the world by joining those groups. Then, when they finally emerge into the world, when they become men again like other men, they are confused and upset. They discover that there are non-Christians in the world who are very much like themselves, who live as they do and as well as they do. And so, they immediately set about trying to discover something that distinguishes them from the rest of mankind. Unfortunately, there are some ill-advised priests who help them by trying to establish, at all costs, some special characteristics which pretend to be the marks of a *visible* superiority. What a waste of time. It is not in being different from men that a Christian is a Christian; it is in being more a man than other men.[2]

In speaking of work, as in speaking of man, we must go beyond the narrow concepts of yesterday; beyond the idea of the 'duties' of one's state in life and of 'offering up' a job well done before and after the fact, so as to render homage to God or to give a meaning to something that essentially has no meaning of its own. We must go beyond the idea of work as an expenditure of energy which does not concern God directly, but which we offer in much the same way that a child offers to his father an ash tray that he has made and which has no value other than that which paternal love attaches to it. And we must come to accept the fact that it is in the act of work itself that man must encounter God.

Obviously, we are talking about an ideal situation. Christians today are not accustomed to living their professions in that perspective. Nevertheless, we must learn to see our work in that light; and we must meditate at length on the active presence of the Risen Jesus in the *whole* of creation. For Jesus is actively present in the smallest particle of matter, in the faintest palpitation of

[2]We should bear in mind that it is only after having studied all aspects of the Mystery of Christ that we can understand how only a Christian can *consciously* live, in their totality, all the dimensions of his own life and of the life of the world.

life. And the worker who touches, with his hand or mind, that particle, who takes and develops and directs that spark of life, encounters therein the creative action of God and the eternal plan of the Father which is mysteriously realised in Jesus Christ.

Man, however, does not encounter Jesus only when he works directly, as an individual, on created matter. He also encounters him, as we shall see, in that work which is the immense collective undertaking of the whole of humanity in its struggle to master the universe, to develop it, and to place it at the service of mankind.

If man is to encounter God in his own work and in mankind's conquest of the universe, it is necessary that two 'projects'—his own and God's—meet in harmony in Jesus Christ. It is necessary that man's will and God's conform to the same end. And it is at that level that there develops either collaboration between the Creator and the co-creator, or a dramatic divorce between the two. It is there, too, that man first experiences God's invitation to a life of intimate union with Jesus Christ in his daily life. It should be clear, then, that only laymen who live in the midst of the world can enjoy the authentic experience of this particular spirituality. And it is equally clear that priests and religious, as they are *today*, are incapable of counselling and guiding laymen in this form of mysticism unless they are willing to forget the classic spirituality they have learned, and unless they are willing, humbly, to contemplate the life and the activity of their layman-brother and to discover therein Jesus Christ—Jesus Christ living already in a place to which they thought they would be able to 'bring' him.

'You must put God into your lives,' the priests used to tell us. They were mistaken. God *is* in our lives. Our job is to find him there, to accustom ourselves to seeing him a bit more clearly every day, to learn to make out his creator-design in our lives so that we may work with him for its fulfilment.

As man works, as he educates himself, as he educates and teaches other men, how can he know that he is working in accordance with the wishes of God and that he is accomplishing what the Father has planned from all eternity? How can he know that, in the midst of his activity, he can encounter and unite himself to Jesus Christ, in whom creation continues according to that eternal plan? In order to answer that question, we will first make a few preliminary remarks. And then we will set out the four criteria in which all others are contained: man's universal climb upward; the mastery and development of the universe for the service of humanity; the free and responsible participation of every man, according to his abilities, in that difficult but exhilarating task; and, finally, the fact that such participation must be accomplished collectively and fraternally by all men on the face of the earth.

Before we can understand what is involved in the integral development of man, we must understand what we mean by 'human development'; and, more basically, we must know what a man is. These definitions are all-important. What is a perfectly constituted, balanced, and developed man? What is involved in living as a man, as a couple, as the member of a community? What is meant by 'working as a man', by relaxing, by participating in the life of society? All of our sciences should be turned to the task of finding the answers to these questions. They should take an inventory of nature, as it were, in order subsequently to be able to develop its resources and channel them to where they are needed, and also to be able to correct nature when necessary (for nature too has been affected by sin). We must not fear to carry out the most painstaking and detailed research on man himself, for, in doing so, mankind—Christians and non-Christians alike—are working in accordance with the wishes of the Father for his children. Jesus Christ accompanies man on his pilgrimage to the sources of this knowledge. If man is faithful to him, he cannot go astray.

The Church, because she knows Jesus Christ, the perfect man, is an expert on mankind; that is, she perceives the direction in which man must grow. And, from time to time, she recalls that direction to man. When that happens, our men of science should take their cue from her. For there can be no contradiction between their discoveries and the thought of the Church (obviously, I am speaking about the Church, and not about churchmen). There can be, of course, difficulties and hesitations along the way, before final conclusions are reached; but that should come as no surprise to anyone, for man's greatness consists not only in working unceasingly for his own development but also in searching out, step by step, what he is and what he must become. The road we must travel is sufficiently well lighted for us to be able to follow it without fear.

1. *The universal ascent of man and of humanity.*

When a man and a woman want to have a child, they invariably want certain things for that child. They would like him to be big and handsome, intelligent, educated— an artist, even; they want him to be talented, a 'doer', efficient, successful in life; and they want him to be a good man. And when they have a child, finally, which they create in love, they do everything possible to assure that he will become what they want him to be.

It is not likely that the heavenly Father is less loving than earthly fathers. Man is the masterpiece of creation because God has wanted him to be such. God has made man in his own likeness, because he wanted man to be greater and more beautiful than we could have imagined until Jesus Christ revealed it to us. Even before Christ, the Psalmist was able to write: 'Ah, what is man that you should spare a thought for him, the son of man that you should care for him? Yet, you have made him a little less than a god, you have crowned him with glory and splendour, made him lord over the work of your hands, set all things under his feet' (*Ps.* 8:4–6).

What God the Father has dreamed of for his sons, he wishes to see come true. And so, he 'raises' each one of us in such a way that we may attain *total* development. He wants man to be fully developed, to be a 'complete man', in body and soul and in all aspects of his life both natural and supernatural. We must be wary, of course, of confusing the levels of man's existence; but, at the same time, we must avoid the temptation to cut man into slices and, even more, to place the resulting pieces in opposition to one another. In man, it is impossible truly to develop one aspect of his being or of his life to the detriment of another aspect. For that reason, certain schools of spirituality are gravely in error. For example, true Christian 'detachment', as we shall see, is never a refusal to participate in life; instead, it is the will to live more fully, to be more truly man. No withdrawal from life can be 'for the glory of God'; on the contrary, withdrawal is an insult to God, for it constitutes the rejection of a gift which God means to be used. Man has no more right to mutilate his mind than he has to mutilate his body. For that reason, the chastity of the celibate must never be a psychological castration. The celibate must not simply renounce the use of his sexual forces; he must use them at another level of existence. Every man, whoever he is and whatever his state in life, must communicate life. Not to do so—to prevent life from flourishing and flourishing 'humanly'—is, simply, abortion.

Sacred Scripture does not recognise the separation between flesh and spirit, body and soul. It is not possible to conceive of the human body without its principle of life. It is true that, in studying man, we make a distinction between the animating spirit and the animated body; but we must never lose sight of the fact that man is neither an angel nor a beast, but, in the unity of his person, is Man.

Too many Christian laymen and priests have attempted to 'disincarnate' man. The attitudes with which they operate have indeed become so deeply rooted that they have passed into everyday language. A pious and zealous pastor will say that his parish comprises three thousand 'souls', or that so-and-so is a 'good soul'. The old adage to the effect 'I have only one soul to save' should be condemned, not only because of the individualistic approach to salvation which it expresses, but also because of the false view of Christianity and of Christians which it reveals. It is *all* of man, the whole man, that Christ came to save; because it is *the whole man* whom God loves and whom he invites to the prodigious and final drama of the resurrection. It is the whole man whom the Father, eternally loving, wishes to see grow in time. God cannot bear to see an underdeveloped man, be he underdeveloped voluntarily or through indifference or through the fault of others, regardless of whether it is a matter of physical,[3] intellectual, or moral underdevelopment. For each and every man,

---

[3]Sickness itself is always an evil. It is not 'wanted' by God; and we should not 'resign ourselves' to it. We should instead fight sickness with all the resources at our disposal. And in that battle—as we shall see when we speak of the mystery of the Redemption—Christ is our companion in arms.

God wants, and has always wanted, *integral* development.

We, for our part, should, in Jesus Christ, fulfil God's desires in our regard. We should develop a hundredfold the gifts he has given us. Man, unfinished, is an insult to God; but the complete man is God's glory. Thus, everything that leads to human development is in harmony with that creative process which takes place in Jesus; and, through Jesus, God is present in it. I mean that man, whether he knows it or not, is working with Christ when he works, on his behalf or on that of all mankind, for physical and spiritual health, for greater liberty, for interior harmony and unity, for more equilibrium within himself, for greater mastery over himself, for more understanding and knowledge, for a greater ability to communicate with other men, for more control over nature, and so forth.

Man, as an individual, does not develop solely through his own resources. He makes use also of those of all other men, individually and collectively, as a member of a group and of a society. He makes use, too, of the economic, political, and social structures of mankind. And Jesus Christ is present in all those men and, through them, in all those structures, in so far as they are useful in man's upward climb. Thus, because the Father desires the spiritual development of man—not only the acquisition of knowledge, but the expansion of all his faculties—we must believe that Jesus is present in all schools and colleges, in the work of the students and their teachers, in the election of class officers, and in meetings of parent-teacher associations. He is present in day nurseries and in graduate schools; in schools for retarded children and in institutes for higher learning; in governmental departments of education and in the legislative bodies that pass laws affecting the educational process. Jesus is present in all men, in all organisations, in all structures. For it is the complex of all these efforts, of all this competency and generosity (and also of all incompetency and selfishness) which speeds or retards or impedes man along the road to self-development according to the plan of the Father. Everything is related in space and in time. A teacher owes his knowledge to his own teachers; he makes use of books written by others; he owes his education, perhaps, to the fact that, many years before, other men had passed laws making education compulsory. When a boy gets his high school diploma, or a young man obtains a college degree, it is because a collective effort of men, both yesterday and today, has allowed him to become, intellectually, what he should be.

If this is true of one aspect of human development, it is true also of all other aspects. When man grows in one of his dimensions, it is because of God, who daily creates him; but it is also because of the work of all other men. St John tells us (1:3) that 'not one thing had its being but through him.' We may add that not one thing has its being but through the whole of mankind.

It is not a single person, but the whole of humanity that must reach a state of complete development. God has not created special classes of men. Everyone, without exception, receives at birth the basic right to physical and spiritual well-being. And everyone, according to his abilities, has a right to maximum development. Not to attain that development because of one's own laziness is a grave fault; but to deprive someone else of it through selfishness is a monstrous injustice. We should suffer when we see an unfinished man. We should blush and ask for forgiveness in the face of that multitude of underdeveloped men whom society has crushed and despised. God has not willed these things. We can be sure, to the contrary, that God, in Christ, is present in everything that concerns the intellectual development of man—in the struggle of student organisations for the democratisation of education, in the workings of scholarship committees and student-loan committees; and also in classes for 'slow-learners', in neighbourhood schoolrooms where volunteers teach immigrants to read and write, in trade schools, in the elementary education movement in Brazil, in the work in UNESCO, in everything everywhere.

If a Christian is satisfied with himself, with his little personal devotions, his little domestic world; if he does not become involved, according to his situation and his gifts, in man's great effort to rise, then that Christian has rejected the work of Christ, who, as the emissary of the Father, is in the process of creating a total humanity from which to forge his mystical Body.

We men have atrophied that mystical Body of Christ, not only because of our poverty in the order of grace, but also (and previously—in so far as we can speak of a 'before' and an 'after' in this context) because we have impeded the natural growth of the members of that body; and we have done this either out of laziness or selfishness, or worse, because of a distorted concept of a disincarnate 'supernatural order'.

We cannot say that we belong to Christ if we are not passionately involved—yes, even to the laying down of one's life—in man's upward ascent; for mankind is the cherished offspring of the Father, whom God has so loved that he sent his only Son among men in an act of ineffable love.

2. *The mastery and development of the universe for the benefit of man.*

God, as we have noted, gave the earth—that is, the universe—to man so that he might reign over it and subject it to himself. It is only a short time since man has begun really to dominate nature. Before that, he was occupied mostly with defending himself against natural forces and with struggling to feed and clothe himself adequately. There was little question of 'mastering nature'. Today, however, he is working toward that mastery—beginning with that tiny particle of matter which is his body, and then reaching out toward the land, the sea, and the universe, which he is just beginning to explore.

In this new role, man no longer functions as a workman alone in his shop, but as a member of a group, with his brothers. And slowly, sporadically, but irreversibly, he is achieving the liberation—individual and collective—of mankind. This is the beginning of the task that God entrusted to man at the beginning of time. And man is entering into a new age.

Why should man dominate nature? The answer is simple: to place nature at the service of man, for the benefit of all men. But nature, or the universe, if it can be the occasion for human growth, can also crush man. It can be inadequately controlled. Or, if controlled, it can be used to obtain only what is immediately useful; and thus, it can render man once more its servant rather than its master by making him dependent upon it for material goods—so dependent that man would do anything to obtain those goods, even at the expense and to the detriment of his brothers, whom he would be willing to transform into slaves, and thus into enemies. Such, unhappily, are the disadvantages of unbridled capitalism, of that 'consumer society' against which young people today, in so many countries are in violent revolt, even though they may be the submissive beneficiaries of such a system, and later become, like their elders, its slaves.

We must not conclude from this, however, that it is

wrong for the earth, through man's efforts, to produce more and more goods; wrong for the material standards of life slowly to be rising; wrong for men to be becoming richer in 'consumer goods'. What is wrong is that a few men 'capitalise' unjustly on the wealth of all mankind, to the detriment of the rest of humanity, and that many men become dependent upon wealth rather than dominating wealth and using it for purposes of spiritual growth.

It is not a matter of having to choose between *having* more and *being* more. The two are not incompatible. But we must be careful that having more does not exclude, but encourages, our being more.

Nature, once subdued by man, can not only be used in other ways than for man's benefit, may not only make of man a perpetually dissatisfied and selfish hedonist, but it can also be used by man against other men. We have not far to look for examples. Think for a moment of the vast treasure of money, intelligence, imagination, and energy that nations have expended, and continue to expend, in a deadly arms race. If God gave the earth to man, it was surely not with the intention that man should use it to kill his brother.

We have said that it is work, human effort, which characterises man's struggle in time and space to subdue nature; and it matters little whether we speak of intellectual work or manual work, scientific work or artistic work. God, since the creation of man, has intended that man work. And every man should work; for work is one of the essential vocations of humanity. Moreover, every man has the right to work, not only in order to support himself and his dependants, which is one of the consequences of work, but also—and more importantly—in order to become a complete man; that is, to become co-creator, with Jesus Christ and all other men, of the work. Man becomes more fully man by means of work freely undertaken and performed. (That is a fact which Marxists know almost intuitively.) Work is not a punishment, but an honour. It has become difficult because of sin—'With sweat on your brow shall you eat your bread' (*Gen.* 3:19)—but it retains its essential dignity. Work is one of the Christian mysteries.

Great masses of humanity, unfortunately, have been excluded from that mystery. They have no work. Others— the majority—work, but they are so poorly remunerated that they can hardly support themselves and their families, and they have become slaves rather than free and responsible workers. God has not willed this; and he does not will it now. In Jesus, God strives for the liberation of all workers; and when men strive to free themselves, they can —if they know it and if they wish it—go forward consciously, in the midst of the battle, to meet their Saviour. Let us remember the enormous effort expended, the great sufferings endured, and the blood shed, on behalf of the labour movement. Let us become as aware of the problems of an apprentice's first day on the job as we are of union meetings, strike votes, labour legislation, and the international labour movement as a whole. Let us be mindful of the vast army of labourers on the move throughout the world and in history. And then let us ask God to let us see these things through his eyes. Then we will not be tempted to oversimplify the problems, quickly to divide mankind into the exploiters and the exploited, automatically to canonise any demand of labour unions. Then, freed from our hidden fears, rid of our traditional middle-class ideas, with our hearts parified, we will discover—through and beyond love and hate, truth and error, sin and grace—the great battle of militant labour to realise the eternal plan of the Father: to accomplish the mastery and development of the universe for the benefit of mankind, to raise this man,

and all men, to the level of his divine vocation as co-creator
of the universe in freedom, pride, and the full development
of his faculties.

3. *The free and responsible participation of every man according
to his abilities.*

Man was not the first to claim for himself the responsibility for his life in all its aspects; he was not the one who discovered the concept of participation. It was God. From the
very first pages of the Bible, God expressed his confidence
in man by giving him a world—not, however, a ready-
made world, but one which remains to be built; not a
completed and perfect humanity, but a humanity which is
still to be created. This was not the act of a benevolent
employer toward his workers. God is the Father; but he
is not paternalistic. No employer, certainly, would leave
it to his workers to decide when they would work and
what they would work on. No employer would place all
of his own resources and all of his power at the disposal of
his workers so that they might decide their goals for themselves and work toward those goals. God's world is not a
Meccano set; it does not come with instructions for
assembly. It is raw material, which has been placed in the
hands of free men.

Man's job is to complete humanity. God has given him
complete responsibility for the job. Men know that, sooner
or later, it will be up to them to decide whether to give
or withhold life. A man has a child. Will he have a second
child? He has two; does he want a third? God will bend to
man's will. He has infinite respect for human freedom,
which is the apex of responsibility. It is an act of folly
of divine love, by which God places the destiny of creation
into the hands of man.

Throughout the world today, man seems to be awakening from a long sleep. Everywhere, among all social classes, in all nations, under all political regimes, men—the young first, and then the adults—are beginning to rediscover, albeit confusedly, their basic dignity. They have come to realise that they too can attain happiness, find joy in life. They sense that they too can become *responsible participants* in the whole of life, whether it be in school, in the factory, or in the office—or in any sector of the political, economic, and social worlds. They are no longer content to be given something to eat when they are hungry, to be given work when they are unemployed, to be allowed to go to school when they are illiterate, to be allowed to develop their countries when the latter are underdeveloped. What they all want is to be free, and to be the masters of their own destiny. And when they have enough to eat, when they can find work, and when they can go to school, what they want is not a higher salary, or a refrigerator, or a washing machine, or even an automobile. What they want is to be responsible. What they are demanding is more than physical or intellectual food and more than material well-being. They demand their dignity as men. But very few men know that what they are really asking for, in effect, is that they be allowed to become what God has always wanted them to be.

The collective awakening that we see in the world today is the expression of an uneasiness, a sense of surprise, the revolt of an adolescent who suddenly discovers that he has become a man after having been told for years that he was still a child. The disorder and suffering which that awakening implies are the first, painful contractions which must precede the birth of a new world.

There are certain men who reject, out of hand and without due consideration, anything which seems to them to be an obstacle, either proximate or remote, to this vindication and development of their being. Therefore, many of those at every level of society who hold positions of responsibility become frightened and attempt to hold on to the *status quo*. They are wrong to do so, for it is wrong to attempt to stifle just and reasonable aspirations. Such aspirations must be recognised and oriented toward a constructive goal. To do otherwise is a waste of energy for society, and an impediment to man's evolution toward maturity.

First in the order of execution, we must try to understand in depth this movement of dissent. And we must not try to suppress it, or to neutralise it by attempting to appease those who are contesting the *status quo* by smothering them in material advantages. An abundance of pocket money may satisfy a child, but its equivalent cannot satisfy a man. Alms, in whatever form, even if necessity compels one to accept them, constitute a humiliation; and, later on, this humiliation will increase tenfold the bitterness of the recipient's demands for justice. To create a welfare society is to create a revolutionary society, whether we are speaking of individuals or of nations as a whole. What people want is no longer merely to be handed 'benefits' by society. They want participation and responsibility within the framework of society; and, more exactly, they want a just sharing of responsibility.

Many of today's angry men realise that they have been deprived by their brothers of those responsibilities, and even of goods which were intended for them. God may have given the earth to all men; but many men have never been allowed to benefit from that gift. A privileged few have taken it and kept it for themselves and made capital on it; these men—perhaps they are more enterprising than other men, or more unscrupulous, or more intelligent, or more audacious—have monopolised that gift and turned it into profit for themselves. They forget that the earth is the possession of all men; that it belongs to everyone, both individually and collectively, and that everyone has a right to a share in it. The earth is not shared on a basis of first come first served; nor does it belong to the hardest worker, or to the most virtuous, or to the strongest. The law of the strongest, above all, is not the law of God.

There are men who exercise responsibility and who justify excluding others from a similar exercise by saying, 'They would not be able to do it, to think, to give orders, to work.' We may ask, then, whether a newborn infant is able to walk. What would we think about parents who, in order to keep the child from falling, would force him to stay in bed forever, and then say, 'Well, he has nothing to complain about. We give him enough to eat.' Such parents would soon be hauled up in court, for they would have committed a crime. They would, in effect, have killed their child; for they would have destroyed the man that that child was destined to become. There is not more than one principle of justice, and that principle applies to all cases. If a man does not yet possess that which God has offered to him of the world's goods and responsibilities, then he has a duty to fight until he obtains them. And if what he has received from God's hands has been taken away by human hands, then he has a right to take it back. Moreover, God will help him in his struggle to regain it.

Thus, everything that works toward that conquest, or re-conquest, of the goods of the earth works within the context of God's plan. It matters little whether we are talking about the possession of a house which a man can call his home, or about the land on which a farmer works, or about the responsibility of a student in his courses or of a worker in his job or of a citizen in his community. Everything that

serves as an inspiration, a search, or a battle for the establishment of an economic, political, and social system within
which all men, each according to his abilities, may have a
share in the collective responsibility of mankind for the
development of the universe—all this is within God's
plan. And Jesus, too, is there, waiting for man so that he
may fight side by side with him.

4. *Collective and fraternal participation by all the men of
the world.*

God, as we have said, has not given each individual man
the responsibility for building up the world. He has given
it to all men, collectively. No one man, therefore, can
accomplish that task by himself, without the help of other
men.

Man, like it or not, is bound to all men on the face of
the earth; and he is even more closely bound to those
who live in proximity to him. In order to develop himself,
he has need of everyone, just as everyone else has need
of him. He is one member of a great body. The function of
grace is to transform, to divinise, the natural solidarity of
that body, which is humanity; it is, in other words, to
build up the Body of Christ.

Man must not only recognise the existence of that solidarity; he must also accept it, and, even more, live it in
love. Those who do so act in accordance with God's will,
who, from the very beginning, established in nature the
roots of human brotherhood. Jesus Christ came on earth to
activate that brotherhood. Man, therefore, is able to unite
himself to Jesus' work. A student, for example, does not
study and work alone. Within Jesus, he is united with the
others in his class, with everyone living in a scholarly
milieu, with other young people in his own country and
all over the world. Workers, likewise, whether rural or

urban, are one with their brothers who do the same kind of work, and indeed with the whole of the world of labour.

In other words, every man has the grave and difficult obligation to reconcile the necessity of personal growth with the necessity of not growing alone. He can achieve this unity only by working, with all his resources and with all other men, beginning from the place in which he finds himself, to build up the world. It is in accomplishing this act of creation that man completes himself and attains happiness. He can never be fully and truly happy without other men; for God has permanently united in Jesus Christ the destiny of the world and the destiny of all men and of humanity.

The over-all conclusion we may draw from the above is this, that we must believe in the world. Whether we wish to believe it or not, the whole of creation—this creation which, within us and under our very eyes, is continuing and working toward completion and perfection; this creation which is the very life of man, humanity, and the universe—is not merely 'profane'. Its trademark, as it were, is divine; for it is the product of God's eternal love in his Son. It is an act of love, yesterday and today and tomorrow, for it is being created by God every day. And it is a continuing and insistent appeal to man from God, an invitation to work freely in the vineyard of the world; and thus, it is an invitation also to a divine intimacy the dimensions of which are incalculable.

Because a Christian believes in heaven does not mean that he should not believe in the world. On the contrary. In contemplating his transcendent God in his uncreated Love, the Christian discovers the source of creation. He should admire it, marvel at it, be proud of it infinitely more than the non-Christian. The non-believer can marvel only at a river whose course is too often broken and whose waters are too often polluted; he cannot know the pure source of all things. Much more than the non-Christian, therefore, the believer should believe in the unprecedented development of the earth, and he should take pride in it. He must not tamely acquiesce in things as they are, for he knows that the lengthy process of evolution—man's prodigious leap from the caverns to scientific accomplishment, from being the victim of nature to the unbelievable accomplishments of technology, science, and industry—which has overcome all obstacles and failures and won many battles, is but the unfolding in time of a work common to God and to man, as Creator and co-creator.

Christians declare that they believe in 'the resurrection of the body'. But no one can separate the body from the air, the sun, and the earth which enable the body to live. The universe itself is but the total body of mankind, of which man is the animating principle, the mover. The whole of creation, therefore, will 'enjoy the same freedom and glory as the children of God' (*Rom.* 8:21). There will indeed be 'a new heaven and a new earth' (*Rev.* 21:1).

No one knows, of course, if this entry of the earth into glory will take place in historical continuity with the existence of the present-day earth and present-day humanity. It seems improbable. St Paul (1 *Cor.* 15:36) says, in speaking of the resurrection, that 'whatever you sow in the ground has to die before it is given new life.' Perhaps it will be the same for the earth. But it makes little difference. We Christians believe that our own bodies will become 'incorruptible'—or, as Paul says (1 *Cor.* 15:54), that they will 'put on imperishability and . . . immortality.' In the same way, we believe that it is our very own world, the world that we ourselves will have developed, which will be transformed into 'a new earth'. If a seed has to die (to continue Paul's analogy), it is of the greatest importance that it be a seed of much beauty and goodness, so that those qualities may be reproduced tenfold in the plant that is to rise up in triumph. For the flower is wholly contained in the seed which is planted.

The Christian, more than anyone else, should believe most fervently in the earth. He alone can grasp, through the knowledge of faith, the mystery of creation in all its breadth and depth—in its totality. He alone is aware of the infinite dimension of the earth's origin, expansion, and development. He, above all, should be filled with joy at this mystery, with knowledge, and with enthusiasm.

Why is it, then, that Christians so often seem eager to place themselves apart from the world? Why do Christians fear the world? Why are they suspicious of it? No doubt, there is always the danger that one will be led astray by the world and monopolised by it. Nevertheless, when a Christian withdraws, even partially, from mankind's struggle to conquer the world, he does not do so because of his faith; he does so because he lacks faith.

What is true of creation in general is even more true of man in particular. God has always had man in his heart. He gives a sign of that presence when he creates and develops man. That creation is not the sort of single and final act by by which a mother gives birth to a child; it is rather the act of a parent who continues always to give birth to that child. Man can therefore find God in himself, in the depths of his own being and his own existence and in the existence of all men. God is the source within us of that river of life from which we take our own lives. God is Love, and man is an act of that Love-made-flesh. When we take pride in our lives and in those of our brothers, we take pride in God. When we love our lives and those of all men, it is God whom we love and whom we glorify. When we abandon ourselves to life in order that life may be improved, we are, in fact, abandoning ourselves to the Creator. If there is a danger in all this, it is not that man will be too much loved or defended or developed; it is instead the danger that man will be badly loved, or—even more—not loved enough. The longer a Christian lives, the more he should love man; and the more he loves man, the more he will grow to love God, the Creator of man.

Creation, as the continually engendered child of the Father, must take cognisance of this relationship and, each day, make an act of love to the Father. But alone and unaided, creation cannot do so. At the apex of the created order, however, at the pinnacle of matter and of life, there is spirit and freedom in the person of man. And man, the fruit of the world, a product of the earth to which he is indissolubly joined, the free co-creator with God of mankind and of the universe, can offer himself to God. He can offer also man's universal climb to the heights, and the universe which man has conquered, transformed, and developed but which, of itself, has not the quality that would enable it to recognise its own beauty, or the mouth to give thanks to God, or the heart to love God.

On the altars of our churches, a candle, lighted in love, glorifies God. In our ceremonies, incense of human offering rises toward heaven in praise and homage. But before the liturgy of the Church there is the immense liturgy of the universe in the process of completion. The candle of this liturgy is the factory chimney which rises above the city, and its incense is the luminous trail left by jets in the sky. The candles and incense of the churches have value as offerings to God only to the extent that they are offered with love. But the factory chimney and the jet have a significance of their own; they represent and embody man's historical effort to participate in the work of God the Creator—and that work is the creation of the world which continues to take place in the sight of God and man.

May there be Christians who are fully men at the centre of that sacred undertaking! Christians who will carry that work forward to its completion in Christ, so that, together with him, they may carry it beyond time and beyond death to place it finally into the hands of God.

May there be in the world a new army of men like Francis of Assisi, Christians who are fully citizens of the world! Men who will not only sing hymns of praise to creation, but also, having transformed and renewed creation, offer it to God—offer it as a prize made rich by the human mind, increased by man's blood, marked by human brotherhood, and afire with the struggle for greater human dignity and freedom.

It is man who is the worker of creation and the priest of creation. All things are his. But he is Christ's; and Christ is God's.

6. The Mystery of the Incarnation

'The Word was made flesh.' What more is there to say? God, in the person of his Son, came to earth to enter into and to assume the totality of human nature. He came in the body of a man, with the heart of a man, to live a human life. God became God-Man.

We know, however, that there is unity in the universe and in humanity. Men are members of a body, which is called mankind; and the universe itself is but an extension of that body. We cannot separate a man from his father and mother, and these latter from their parents, and their parents from their own parents. . . . Man is bound to all other men. If he is to become fully man, he must accept all men as his brothers. But he must go beyond that. He must communicate with them in a spirit of love. To believe otherwise is to say that a hand can be a real hand apart from the body.

It is likewise impossible to separate man from the universe, for man cannot live without the earth, the air, and the sun. Man sprang from the earth, and he is brother to the earth. He needs the earth in order to be born, to live, and to grow. There is nothing in creation that man does not need—'not a star in the heavens,' as Paul Claudel declared.

God, because he became man in Jesus Christ, takes to himself, by virtue of that humanity, all men of every time and every place. And, less obviously (but none the less truly), he also takes to himself all of the universe. By divinising man, Christ will achieve the final unity of the human race in the likeness of the Trinity: 'That all may be one, as

you and I are one.' Jesus willingly accepts the bond which
unites him to man. He came through love; and it is through
love that he encounters and unites himself to those who,
henceforth, are to be his brothers. In Jesus Christ, God
communicates with all men, so that all men may communicate with him.

The first act of communication between man and God
took place through Mary, and it was in Mary that that act
was accomplished. In her, as the embodiment of the
highest human perfection which had been prepared from
the beginning of the world, all men and all of the earth
were brought into the presence of God; and God was
brought into the presence of man and of the world. Mary's
'yes'—a total and efficacious affirmative—was in her and
through her the first 'yes' of mankind to the uniting of
Creator and creature, of the 'natural' and the 'supernatural'.

Since man, in Mary, had given his assent, God came; and
he thereby fulfilled his promise and sealed the alliance. He
came, as a man among men; and because he was wholly
man and infinitely loving, he came to enter into every man,
into all of humanity and the world, through the presence
of his love. That is the Event which dominates history. It
is the realisation and accomplishment of the Father's eternal
plan of love: to 'bring together . . . everything in the
heavens and everything on earth' (*Eph.* 1:10).

The coming of Christ among men two thousand years
ago is the visible expression of a unique and eternal act of
love which unfolds in time and space, beginning with the
creation of the universe and enduring until the coming of
triumphant Christ at the end of the world. For the incorporation of all mankind into Christ must take place
gradually, step by step, at the same tempo as man, a

wanderer in history, says his 'yes' as an act of love. Christ does not compel love, and he does not unite himself to a man who is unwilling.

Love is, in effect, a giving and a taking, and that giving and that taking are inseparable. A man who gives, or even gives himself, but forgets or refuses to take, is simply indulging in an act of paternalism. Love presupposes an exchange; that is, it presumes that one person be, with respect to another person and at the same time as that other person, sufficiently wealthy to give and sufficiently poor to take.

Man, moreover, limited as he is—among other reasons, because of his existence in time—cannot give himself definitively to another by a unique act of love. That love takes place in time; it is developed in time. Lovers say 'yes' to one another on a particular day, and they do so in joy and in full liberty. By their mutual 'yes,' they commit their lives and their eternity, for that affirmative contains all other affirmatives. And the lovers marry. But then, they must set about becoming in fact that which they are in theory. They must work out their 'yes' in daily life, and live out their commitment. In the same way, man's personal answer to God is given within the context of each man's concrete existence, day after day. The 'yes' of Jesus to mankind, on the other hand, is perfect and complete; it is at once a total gift from God to man, and the expression of a willingness, an openness, to man's love, to the degree that man is willing to give it. That willingness of man, however, that act of consenting, can only take place step by step. Man makes himself man every day, and he should make himself a Christian every day; that is, he should surrender himself, his life, and the life of the world, to love, and thus allow Jesus Christ to make real for him, in time and in humanity, what he has already accomplished once and for all.

It is in this sense that we can say the mystery of the Incarnation is not yet complete. No doubt, the advent of God in a man's body and in human life—i.e., the physical or historical Incarnation—is complete. But the mystical Incarnation, Jesus' coming into each man, into man's life and the life of the world, even though it has been perfectly accomplished in the love of Christ, must still be realised in time by means of man's free response.

'I am the vine, you are the branches,' said Jesus. 'Make your home in me, as I make mine in you' (*John* 15 :4–5). But just as not all of the vine's branches reach maturity, so too not all men are one with Christ; not all men 'make their home' in him.

Christ is the head and we are the members. 'If we live by the truth and in love, we shall grow in all ways into Christ, who is the head by whom the whole body is fitted and joined together, every joint adding its own strength, for each separate part to work according to its function. So the body grows until it has built itself up, in love' (*Eph.* 4:15–16). But that body is not yet complete. Each day, it grows.

Christ is the cornerstone of a holy temple. 'As every structure is aligned on him, all grow into one holy temple in the Lord; and you too, in him, are being built into a house where God lives, in the Spirit' (*Eph.* 2:21–22). But the building is not yet over. The temple has not yet been constructed.

The mystical Incarnation of Christ is realised simultaneously in two 'dimensions': in 'depth' and in 'breadth'. In depth, Jesus Christ establishes contact with man and seeks his response in love. Such is the mystery of communication and identification between Christ and the Christian, until the latter is totally transformed by Christ, until he becomes a new man in a new life, so that he may say with St Paul, 'It is now not I who live, but Christ who lives in me'.

History, then, is nothing more than Jesus' continuing act of love in quest of man; his enduring declaration of love, spoken in the depths of the heart and of being; his permanent desire to incorporate all men into himself so that they may become, in him, sons of the Father and brothers among themselves.

There is only one success that is possible for man. There are not two, a 'human' one for the world and a 'divine' one for the Church. And that single, unique success consists in being divinised. That is the end, the total development, that God has always desired for man. God has made man 'incorporable' in his very being; therefore, man can be truly man only in becoming a Christian of Christ and in Christ.

By extension, we may say that Jesus takes to himself all of mankind, and, through mankind, all of the universe. And thus, mankind collectively—man in his natural communities, in his nations, in his Church—must give an answer to Christ's love, until all men are joined together in the unity of faith in, and knowledge of, the Son of God— that is, 'until we become the perfect Man, fully mature with the fullness of Christ himself' (*Eph.* 4:13). 'And when everything is subjected to him, then the Son himself will be subject in his turn to the One who subjected all things to him, so that God may be all in all' (1 *Cor.* 15:28). Thus, the eternal plan of the Father will be realised, 'that he would bring everything together under Christ . . . everything in the heavens and everything on earth' (*Eph.* 1:10).

The mystery of creation unfolds in time, as a gesture of God's love, in Christ. At the heart of that creation, by virtue of man's universal aspirations and his development of himself and of the world through work, there is already a close link between God and man. But, as creation continues, Jesus Christ, by that same gesture of love, gathers it to himself totally. By his Incarnation, he completes it and gives it its final meaning in order to bring it to its supreme accomplishment: the creation of a 'new man' and a 'new earth'. This is the realisation of man's deepest aspirations, of the need to become 'great', to develop more and more—until what? Man does not always know the answer to that 'until what'. But we know that we have a taste for the infinite within ourselves. And, in fact, Christ invites us to rise infinitely above ourselves and to take a new greatness upon ourselves—a greatness which the Father has planned for us from all eternity: divinisation in Christ Jesus. 'Before the world was made, he chose us . . . determining that we should become his adopted sons, through Jesus Christ' (*Eph.* 1:4–5).

Christ tells us who God is, and he tells us who man is—since he himself is wholly both God and man. His purpose in coming is to make of man that which man should be. And all men are, with respect to Christ, in the process of development and of 'humanisation' and divinisation. By incorporating us into himself, Christ allows us to achieve our fullest expansion.

To man's ineradicable desire to build a world of justice, and peace, and happiness which surpasses all previous happiness, there corresponds in Christ a desire to build a world that will reach 'as high as heaven'. For the whole of creation, affected as it is by the redemptive Incarnation of Christ, has received, through man, the promise of eternal life.

If mankind sets its sights low and keeps its own development and that of the world at ground level, then man will never be fully content. Man has a reminder of his divine origin and destiny in the hunger for the infinite which lies in his heart. Men, in other words, need God. If they ignore God, or reject him, then they must necessarily turn to the quest for material goods which are sought for their own sake; for men will then lack *the* supreme Good. They will want to possess everything, because they will lack that which *is* everything. And they will fight, and kill, in order to defend their material possessions. They will glut themselves with 'consumer goods'—goods that they will, quite laudably, have developed, but which they will have perverted by making of them an end in themselves. Man will then allow himself to be dominated, crushed, and destroyed by the dissatisfaction of having created a surface humanity and a surface world—a humanity and a universe that do not attain the infinite depths for which they were intended. They will be plants without fruit, condemned to sterility and to final death.

Jesus Christ did not choose to use heaven as a podium from which to give man directions for the proper use and development of creation; and he did not choose to hand over a detailed set of instructions. Instead, he came down and entered into creation itself, into human flesh and human life, in order to give roots and sap to the plant which is to bear the fruit of eternity. Without Christ, creation would abort.

Henri Bergson used to say that what the world needed was more soul. Today, what the world needs is more love. And it is a matter of life and death.

Human progress is ever increasing its pace. Thousands of centuries were necessary for man to rise above the level of the savage. But only a few centuries were necessary to produce an Einstein. The energy of love, however, does not develop as quickly as the energy of the mind. What will be man's destiny, one wonders, if, as he becomes more and more rich intellectually and more and more attracted to the world which he is developing, he becomes less and less able to achieve unity through love? He will be over-whelmed by the forces he has created—a being who can launch a spaceship and compute its orbit to the tenth of a second, but who cannot master his own nature. Man, if he is too rich in intellect, in emotion, in imagination, but too poor in love, runs the risk of becoming a nothing, a puppet on a string, a shadow of what man should be.

Man's power over nature is growing proportionately to his increasing intellectual energies. It took hundreds of centuries for man to learn to fly, but only a few years for him to learn how to reach the planets. We belong to the generation of men who have discovered the secret of matter and of the energy it contains. Surely, that is something to be proud of. But we also belong to the generation of men who made their first use of that secret in order to kill two hundred thousand of their brothers at Hiroshima. We may well ask what will become of the world, now that it has fallen into the hands of man. Will it revert to a primordial chaos? Will man be forced back into the dawn of time, to begin all over again the work of building up the world? And what of society itself? Under-endowed as it is with love, will it sicken and open itself to the deadly cancer of selfishness and hate? We know now from experience that even the most humane and just of our economic, political, and social institutions are nothing unless they are animated with that same human love which transforms man himself. An old house may be torn down and replaced by a splendid new one; but that does not necessarily change the people who live in it. Society today is being reborn; but it will only be reborn in a better form if there is an increase of love in the hearts of men. Otherwise, the new society will be born dead.

We believe wholeheartedly that only the unifying force of love can harmonise and synthesise and personalise man's inner drives. We believe likewise that only love can unite mankind—only love can tear man's eyes away from his own little possessions and preoccupations to make him throw himself into his brother's arms. Love alone can make it possible for man to build up the universe—not for selfish purposes, and for it to become a bone of contention among men, but for it to be placed at the service of all men. And we believe, finally, that this love is a force which has its source above and beyond man, that it is infinitely above man; that it is, in fact, a Person, who is God incarnated and inserted into the heart of humanity, like yeast into bread, in order to make man rise; that it is Jesus Christ.

It is almost unbelievable that we have not yet studied all the consequences of that Event, which is the coming of Christ on earth. So little do we know, that we often find ourselves in the position of men for whom God has not yet come. Like the men of the Old Testament, we seem still to be waiting. We have no faith in the active presence of that Love which never fails.

Jesus Christ has come. He has allowed himself to be circumscribed by the Incarnation, by a human body, by a place, a country, a race, an era. That expedition into humanity, as it were, carried the assurance of Jesus' active presence in history—'I am with you always; yes, to the end of time'—and the proof of man's total incorporation into Jesus. The Risen Christ sent us his Spirit of Love; and the Holy Spirit has not returned to heaven, but remains on earth, in the heart of man, in a relationship more intimate even than that of man to himself and to other men. That

Love is present in the whole of human history and at every instant of it. And, if man allows, Love will make of that history the sacred history of the People of God en route to the new Promised Land. For all this, God is present. But man is often absent.

Man himself must be present to the infinite Presence in order for Christ to continue his 'descent' into humanity, in order for the Incarnation to be actualised each day in man and, through man, in the world. And he must be present in this way in the very heart of reality. Just as Christ wills to perpetuate his eucharistic presence on earth by means of human bread, so too he wills to make his mystical Body grow by means of the bread of human life. The existential aspiration of modern man is basically healthy. It represents a preliminary and unconscious approach to God. Modern man believes in existence, and sometimes only in existence. Unfortunately, he does not always realise that, within existence, God is waiting for him, and that, in the midst of life, is hidden subsistent total Love. Nevertheless, it is there that man can meet his God. He has no need to look further.

Thus, to keep faith with Jesus Christ we must begin by keeping faith with the realities of daily life. Our first act should be the cultivation of loyalty to ourselves, to our lives, to our community and all the human groupings within which we live, to our relatives, our work, etc. It is there that we have the opportunity to take part in the work of creation and, by our faithfulness to that task, in the continuing Incarnation.

No one is a greater realist than the true Christian. The true Christian is not, as one may think, a man who walks with his eyes fixed on the heavens—who lives 'up in the clouds'. On the contrary, the Christian is a man who has his eyes fixed on the earth and who studies the ways of mankind in the light of faith so as to discover the will of the Father. He searches out the answers to questions: What is my mission? How shall I go about doing it? Who are my collaborators? What are we supposed to accomplish? And these questions pertain not only to one's whole life or to one's general vocation, but also to every week, every day, every instant of one's existence.

We have said that Jesus Christ first came into the world because of Mary's free and loving 'yes'. He continues to come into the world, however, because of *our* free and loving 'yes'. He comes to the place where we are—to us, as unique individuals in a particular situation with our own consciences and our human liberty—to live with us that small part of life which is ours, that small event which is part of the great Event.

Every day, we must choose ourselves anew; every day, we must choose our lives anew—that is, the people who are around us, the places where we are, the things in which we participate. All of that life must become ours; for that life is the 'daily bread' that we must assimilate into ourselves. At the same time, we must offer it to Christ, who asks for it. We must allow Christ to transform it within himself and assimilate it totally so that—with our help—he may actualise the mystery of his Incarnation. For man's free and loving 'yes' to his present life is the key to the mystical Incarnation of Jesus which lies at the heart of creation.

Certainly, not every life can be taken by Christ unto himself. It must be a life which is spent according to the will of the Father; that is, a life spent in the betterment of man and in the building-up of the world. That which goes against the will of the Father—that which is sin—is rejected automatically, like an anti-body, for it can provide no nourishment to the Body of Christ.

Man is saved by his life; not the life that he would like to live, or the life that he dreams of living, but the life that he lives from day to day. Indeed, outside of life, there is no salvation.

Thus, the mystery of the Incarnation—that loving undertaking of Jesus to unite himself to all men, and by him perfectly accomplished from the beginning—is realised now in time, and enriched by our conscious response, in love. Our consent was necessary for this union to take place. Because we grow each day, and because we live in a world which itself is gestating, that consent must be expressed daily in the midst of the process of creation. Nothing, no one, must escape Christ; otherwise, we are in danger of becoming the victims of a deadly imbalance between creation-in-growth and that Love which must permeate creation in order to give it its meaning. And nothing must be taken from Christ to be destroyed or turned away from its true purpose; not a piece of ourselves or of our bodies or of our minds; not an instant of individual and collective lives; not a speck of earth; not a moment of history. All things must be subjected to Christ —with man working, consciously and free, to realise God's plan. All things are sacred in their origin; but all things must be consecrated by man, who has been divinised by Jesus Christ.

There are, however, many Christians who have long been absent from the world. They emigrated to a 'spiritual' universe that they created for themselves, or that was created for them, where they lived in the shelter of moral rules and religious rites which, since they had nothing to do with life, were meaningless in themselves, uninspiring for the faithful, and a scandal and counter-witness for everyone else. Such Christians have become aliens, strangers on earth. They must return to their mother country. They must be naturalised and become men once more.

There can be no real 'spiritual life' unless life itself is lived fully. A Christian who is absent from life is a man who has separated himself from Christ.[1] If he does not enter first into communion with Christ's presence in life, he cannot enter into real communion with Christ's presence in the Eucharist: 'The Word was made flesh; he lived among us' (*John* 1:14).

[1]Obviously, I am talking about a Christian who lives, as we say, 'in the world'. Someone who, by a special vocation, 'leaves the world', is only physically separated from it; he does not flee from life, but chooses an alternative way of being present with his brothers in the construction of the universe. He is present spiritually—directly, we may say, in Christ, in whom man and the world are united.

7. The Mystery of the Redemption

The mystery of Christ's Incarnation cannot be understood or fully lived unless it is joined to the mystery of the Redemption. In fact, the Incarnation of Jesus must be—because of sin—a redemptive incarnation. Therefore, before discussing the Redemption itself and trying to understand how we must live it out in our daily lives, it would be useful to examine the notion of sin and suffering.

Man was created out of love, and for love. His vocation is love—not human love alone, but, beginning with human love and through it and in it, also a love divinised and transfigured by the presence of Jesus Christ. The final purpose is for man, in Jesus Christ, with all other men and in a renewed universe, to love with the love of the Trinity. And that is heaven.

As a product of love, man—along with all of mankind and the whole of the universe—must return God's love. It is man's destiny to do so; and without it he can succeed neither with his life nor with the life of the world.

Since man was made by love, it follows that love has willed man to be free. For there can be no love without freedom. To love someone is to want him to be free; it is to lay down one's life, if necessary, to set him free. But freedom, even though it also is a product of love, is not given as such to man. Only the seed of freedom is planted in the human heart. Man's freedom is a freedom which must be tended and made to grow. And it will grow only through love. Man must be free; but he will be truly free only when he learns to love without reservation. Selfishness imprisons man and makes a slave of him; but love sets him free.

We are not talking about physical freedom, but about that extraordinary and inalienable right that we all have to accept or to refuse, to rebel or to submit, to say yes or no with respect to our lives. And that right is operative no matter what external pressures may be brought to bear, and no matter what internal conditions may prevail. Such is the freedom to love.

Man is invited to love. Of course, he can refuse the invitation. And that is sin.[1] Sin is always a conditional love, a love mingled with self-love, or a simple refusal to love throughout one's life.

Sin is the refusal to commit oneself wholly to the creation of oneself (sloth). It is the deformation of that creation (sensuality). It is the creation of oneself for one's own sake while forgetting about one's brothers (selfishness and pride).

Sin is the refusal to risk one's life in order to give life to another in love, so that the other person may go forward or so that other lives may be lived (the sins of married couples and of families). For to love means to give life to another, or to others.

Sin is the refusal to commit oneself to the creation of the world. And it is the deformation and perversion of that creation by developing it solely for one's own ends (the sins of labour, in the most general sense of that term).

Sin is the refusal to allow God's Love to enter into our

[1]Sin has never been disobedience to a 'rule'. The commandments of the Church, for example, are only signposts on the road of love. They remind us, among other things, that we cannot claim to love God and to be loved by God if we do not take communion—or communicate with God—at least once a year. If one sins, it is not because one disobeys a particular commandment; it is because, in disobeying it, one proves that one does not love.

lives so that he may take control of it, and through it reach our brothers and the world (rejection of Christ and of a relationship with him).

Sin is the refusal to recognise and acknowledge God as the supreme end of each man and all men and of the world. It is the refusal to render homage to God. It is the building of a god for oneself in place of God, by thinking only of oneself, by taking for oneself alone what belongs to other men and to God. It is making oneself the centre of creation, and thereby displacing mankind and the universe and causing imbalance and disorientation in the world.

All these refusals are failures to love. They cause man and the world to lose their direction, and they place them outside the plan of the Father, which is to unite all things in love. There are, in effect, only two great forces in the world. One is the force of expansion toward God and toward others; and that force is called love. The other is the force of withdrawal into oneself; and that force is called selfishness, pride, and all the other names which signify aspects of that egocentric regression.

Because God's plan is a plan of love, which can be realised only through love, man's refusal to participate in that plan 'offends' God in his very being—which is love. Sin is the non-requital of God's love. But, because of the Incarnation, sin also offends God because it affects man. Since Jesus Christ united humanity and divinity within himself, and since through him God has united himself to all humanity by taking mankind to himself in its totality, the rejection of one member of the body of humanity implies the rejection of the Head. If we refuse to love man, then we necessarily refuse to love God: 'Anyone who says, "I love God," and hates his brother, is a liar' (1 *John* 4:20). Jesus himself said so in so many words: 'In so far as you did this to one of the least of these brothers of mine, you did it to me' (*Matt.* 25:40). And he warned us that we would be judged according to the degree that we proved our love for him by loving our brothers for their own sake: I was hungry and you gave me food; I was thirsty and you gave me drink; I was a stranger and you made me welcome . . . in prison and you came to see me' (*Matt.* 25:35). Some will say, 'But Jesus is talking about his own people, about those who accept him and believe in him and consciously follow him'. Nonsense. A father does not distinguish between his children who love him and those who ignore and reject him. Jesus did not attach conditions to his redemption of man through love. As a prisoner of his love, he gives himself to all men, without exception. 'His own people' are all men—men of every time, forever. When there is rejection, it does not come from God. God does not reject man. He cannot. If he did, then he would not be infinite Love. But man is capable of rejecting God.

Love gives to man the one chance that he has to save himself. Man must love God with all his strength; and he must love his fellow men in the same way. Jesus tells us that these two loves are but one love, that they are inseparable.

Men, whether they like it or not, are bound to one another. All of mankind is one unit. Men cannot really be men except to the extent that they are united to other men as members are united to a body. Men, in fact, compose a body: humanity. This human solidarity can have one of two consequences: It can work either to man's benefit or to man's detriment. The member who loves and develops within the body gives life to all the other members. But the member who places obstacles in the way of love destroys himself and weakens the rest of the body as well. All non-love—that is, all sin—affects all of mankind. And that is why, when we confess our sins, we acknowledge them before God and before all men living and dead.

In the same way, man is bound to all of creation, in his being and in his acts. He lives in the universe, and he builds the universe; but he can halt that construction, or deflect it from the purpose for which it was intended. When man does that, he stamps sin, as it were, on the heart of creation. A block of flats, for example, is badly built because the builder has no professional ethics. He skimped on essentials, and used cheap materials in order to make a larger profit. The flats are too small, too noisy, badly laid out, and unattractive. People who come to live in that building will undoubtedly be influenced by their surroundings. If they commit immoral acts, how can we measure their responsibility, compared to the responsibility—the less evident, but none the less real responsibility—of those who were indirectly or directly involved in the construction of the building, and who have carved their own sin into the very walls of the building? Such buildings—and such housing 'developments', such cities, such schools and universities, such factories and offices—condone and multiply the sins of man. And the same holds true, of course, for labour and building regulations, for laws—for all the 'structures' which, at every level, control man's life in society.

Thus, sin—like love—is introduced by man into the heart of all creation. And we may therefore say that creation, whose function is to nourish man and help him in his development, can also become an obstacle and the occasion of man's fall. For that reason, Jesus Christ, through man, must carry the Redemption even into the centre of creation. For creation too must be saved. 'The whole of creation is eagerly waiting for God to reveal his son. It was not for any fault on the part of creation that it was made unable to attain its purpose, it was made so by God; but creation still retains the hope of being freed, like us, from its slavery to decadence, to enjoy the same freedom and glory as the children of God. From the beginning till now the entire creation, as we know, has been groaning in one great act of giving birth' (*Rom.* 8:19–22).

It is often said that men today, and particularly the young, are no longer aware of a sense of individual sin, but that they are more intensely conscious than ever of their responsibility for the collective sins which afflict humanity. This attitude—so long as it does not exclude the recognition of personal faults—is a proof of maturity.

Whence come unemployment, inadequate salaries, slums, illiteracy, the exorbitant rate of infant mortality in some countries, hunger, underdevelopment, war? From selfishness, pride, profiteering—from all the sins of man. All of these things are the results of sin—of sins added one to another and linked one to another; from chain-sinning, as it were. And all of mankind is responsible for these sins.

What is an individual man's responsibility for that tragic collective sin? No one knows. Only God knows, for he alone sees each one of us in our own place within the torrent of yesterday's and today's humanity. He alone knows what we are, and why we are what we are. He alone knows what advantages we enjoy and what problems we face. He alone sees our place and function in the construction of the world, and the degree of our commitment to the brotherhood of mankind. And God alone is able to go beyond our outward behaviour and judge us according to the amount of love that we have.

What we men know, however, is that we have some responsibility. We know that the non-love in our lives never exists in a vacuum, but, by some mysterious process, combines with the non-love of other men to form those horrendous collective sins which are the scourge of mankind. And since we are all responsible together, we must strive together to make up for those sins.

There are two kinds of suffering in the world. There is that suffering which is part of nature itself; and that kind is a mystery. And there is that suffering that man adds and superadds every day to necessary suffering by his sins; and this kind can be explained and understood.

It is true that evil existed in the world even before man took a hand in it. For there is no change in nature, no progress, without struggle and suffering and death. A grain of wheat must split, rot, and die before a new plant can rise. An animal, in order to live and survive, must fight and kill. The earth, and the universe itself, emerged and developed only after incredible upheavals. Creation often seems intent on revenging itself for man's progressive domination of it. Why? I do not know. No one knows. If there were no Jesus Christ, I would rebel at the apparent injustice of it all.

The other kind of suffering—that which man creates for himself—is even worse, more horrible and tragic, for man, because man knows its origins and he knows how it could be avoided. Nevertheless, he sometimes seems to take pleasure in increasing that suffering rather than diminishing it. This is the suffering that sin causes in the world. It is a suffering that ranges from the hurt feelings of a neighbour because of a thoughtless word to the mass slaughter of a nation. In between those two extremes, there are such things as the manifestations of non-love in broken homes, in disrupted communities, in the reduction of labour to virtual slavery, etc. There is no sin so small, so obscure, that it does not produce suffering; for every sin generates disorder where there should be order discord where there should be harmony, selfishness and hate where there should be love: 'Sin entered the world through one man, and through sin death, and thus death has spread through the whole human race because everyone has sinned' (*Rom.* 5:12).

Let us make no mistake about it. There are infinitely more men who die from hunger and war than from earthquakes or natural catastrophes. There are more children who die from lack of the most basic care than from 'natural' diseases. There exists, none the less, a terrible illogic in man by which he, perhaps out of hypocrisy, demands that God explain why there is so much natural suffering in the world; while, at the same time, he ignores completely the suffering that he himself creates every day—suffering which, moreover, he could limit, and then eliminate, through love.

We must not think that God should step in and prevent man from hurting himself. We would not want a God who would turn us into remote-controlled robots by constantly intervening in our lives in order to keep us from doing wrong or hurting ourselves or doing something dangerous —a God who would permit us only to do what is safe, who would choose the path we are to follow and tell us what precautions to take. We would not even want a God who would catapult us out of a car that was about to have a collision, or who would make us miraculously grow wings if our aeroplane was going to crash. No. We want to live dangerously. We want to be free. We want to win—but we want to do it ourselves. And this is not pride. It is the will to be what we are: men. To be men, however, we have need of God's love, and we must ask for that love with all our strength. But that love does not do away with our freedom; instead, it gives us freedom.

A god who is a wonder-worker is not our God. Our God is a Father; which is to say that he is loving, that he loves his children enough to allow them to run the risk of sin and the consequences of sin, that he loves them enough never to allow them to suffer alone.

All suffering is, in itself, evil. It is foolish for us to try to explain suffering by pretending that, somehow, it is good. That would be making excuses for God. Suffering is evil, and it will always be evil. But in 'the new heaven and the new earth' there will be no more suffering and no more death: 'Here God lives among men. He will make his home among them; they shall be his people, and he will be their God; his name is God-with-them. He will wipe away all tears from their eyes; there will be no more death, and no more mourning or sadness. The world of the past has gone' (*Rev.* 21:3–4).

I do not believe that God 'sends us suffering' in order to 'punish us' or 'for our own good'. I cannot believe in a God who is Love and who tortures man to make man better. Sin is indeed punished; but it is man who decides on the punishment. In disrupting creation, he creates severe penalties for himself and his fellow men. There is no need for God to add even more punishment. We sometimes see a small child run away from his mother in the street; the child falls and hurts itself—and the mother spanks the child. The spanking serves no purpose, for the child has already been punished for running away by hurting himself. The mother's reaction is emotional; it is illogical, and an imperfection. God does not act out of emotion, or illogically, or imperfectly. He does not spank his children. On the contrary, he comforts them and helps them to bear the hurt.

I do not approve of those Christians who, prostrated by

suffering, can 'bless the will of God'. We do not need people who are resigned and submissive. We need men; men who will fight against suffering. And when suffering refuses to submit, when evil refuses to change, then man must make use of the grace of Jesus Christ to convert it into good. Thus, useless waste products are thrown into the fire—where they are converted into heat and light.

Even at the purely human level, man can make use of suffering in order to grow. The mountain climber who voluntarily risks his life in an ascent suffers from cold, hunger, fatigue. He arrives at the summit a better man for his effort and his suffering. And if that effort and suffering are such as hardly to be borne, he is changed from the man that he was into a hero. If, on the other hand, he reaches the summit in a helicopter, he reaches his goal—but he remains unchanged. In accepting suffering, man is not asked to do anything which is beyond his strength.

Each one of us has a road to travel, the road of our individual lives. That road is filled with problems. Together, we have a world to conquer. It is by effort and struggle that we can succeed in both tasks. There are always difficulties and resistance, but if we face up to them we will end up better men after the battle than before. God, as we have already said, did not give us a ready-made world, but a world that has to be constructed; and we become men when we build it in the midst of difficulties. A child whose parents remove every difficulty and solve every problem will never become strong; he will never mature. Our God may never spank his children, but neither does he spoil them.

Thus, I do not believe that God *wills* suffering. As in the case of sin, he must allow it, 'unwillingly', in order truly to love his children. He did not make either man or the world

perfect. Man must *become* perfect, even as his heavenly
Father is perfect. And he must struggle so that the world
may become perfect too. But he is not required to struggle
singlehandedly—for it would then be impossible for him
to accomplish anything—but to cooperate with Christ.
For Christ is the final proof that God has not resigned
himself to the existence of suffering. Christ has wholly
committed himself to the fight against suffering and death.
Without Christ, there is only despair. But with Christ,
there is hope and victory. And that is the mystery of the
Redemption.

From all eternity the Father has planned that man be his
son in his Son. It is a unique project. There is no initial
failure, and then a 'making-up'. It is also an original
project, as sin and suffering are original, but it enters into
time through the life and passion of Jesus Christ.

The mystery of the Redemption is the reorientation of
man and the universe, in Christ and by him, in the direction
of his final development—which is divine Love. That is the
last battle, and the victorious battle, of Christ against sin,
suffering, and death, so that man, humanity, and the
universe may attain the goal for which they were created.
The great enemy, therefore, the historical obstacle, is sin;
that is, non-love, suffering, and death.

How can Christ overcome this enemy? It was necessary
that he take upon himself all the sins of man in order to
fight and conquer them. But Christ is infinitely pure; he
can have no part of sin. That is the mystery. But, as before,
love clarifies the mystery.

The man who really loves his wife or his friend loves
without conditions and without reservation. He accepts
the loved one as he is, with all his virtues and all his imper-
fections, and even with his sins if he is a sinner. A lover

does not break with the loved one because the latter sins. Instead, he draws nearer to the sinner, embraces him, welcomes him—and takes his sin upon himself. 'Not only do I not condemn you,' he says, 'but I will help you to bear your sin'. In this way, too, Jesus, united to man, takes our sins upon himself. 'For our sake God made the sinless one into sin', St Paul says (2 *Cor.* 5:21). Not one of our faults is foreign to him, whatever may be our individual sins or those tragic collective sins that we spoke of earlier. Because his love is infinite, because he is united to all men, because he is present by his Incarnation, he accepts for himself man's battle against non-love throughout history. And he does this without ever having sinned himself.

Anyone who has ever experienced disgust for the sins of a friend, and has known the tension of continuing to love him, can imagine Jesus' agony. Cut to the heart by man's sin, but filled with love, he suffered to the point of asking the Father to deliver him from this tragic confrontation. He fell to the ground and sweated blood. But he did not abandon man. He continued to love man. Man is his brother, and Christ did not judge him. Rather, he loved man all the more. He united himself to man and took man's sin upon himself.

It was necessary that Jesus also receive all the suffering of the world—the suffering endured by man for the continuing creation of the world—in order to give meaning to that suffering, and the useless suffering, which is the fruit of sin, in order to reclaim it and put it to use.

How could he do this? His body was not large enough to receive the number of whiplashes that would have been necessary; nor his brow, to take the necessary number of thorns. In his passion, Jesus was tortured and put to death. But he was not more tortured, nor did he die more, than have thousands and thousands of men through the centuries (and, most recently, in the concentration camps of World War II). How, then, could he take upon his shoulders the suffering of all mankind since the beginning of time?

I began to understand the answer one day on Good Friday. I had gone to visit a sick child. The doctor was there, and he had just announced that he would have to do a bit of very minor surgery. We took the child to a window and sat him upon a chair. His mother was at his side, of course, pressed against him. Each time the doctor touched him the child registered pain—and so did the mother. Each time the child groaned, the mother groaned. When the doctor had finished, the child felt sick and had to be put to bed. And the mother felt sick and had to be put to bed. In that instant, I understood: When we love, we suffer with the suffering of the one we love.

That, I think, was the true suffering of Jesus Christ. It was not so much the lashes and the crown of thorns and the carrying of the cross. It was the suffering of love. Jesus, because he has infinite love for all men and is aware of every man, saw, knew, and suffered all of man's sufferings. With the weight of these sufferings on his back, he made the way of the cross. His cross was the wooden cross of the Gospels; but it was also, and above all, the gigantic cross which has been erected at the centre of human history.

When, finally, Jesus was nailed to the cross of wood and suspended between heaven and earth, at the moment when he died the death of a man through love, he took upon himself all the deaths of his brothers. He could not defend himself, for to do so would have been to defend himself against love. He was incapable of not opening his heart to all men. In a very real sense, he was a victim of his own love. His Incarnation was a success. He had incorporated all of humanity into himself. On Calvary, all of mankind was joined together in him. The whole of his Body was nailed to the cross.

Then Jesus, the first of all his brothers, the Son of Man, the Head of the great body of humanity, himself total awareness and total freedom, infinite love, was totally alone. And he grasped all the members of his Body, mankind and the universe, their sins and their sufferings and their death, and with one great cry he gave it all to the Father: 'Father, into your hands I commit my spirit'. It was a spirit enriched with all of humanity, past, present, and future. It was all of man, all of human history, and all of creation, now reoriented by Love toward Eternal Love. It was the redemption of the world.

Three days afterwards, the Father gave life back to his Son—his own life, and the life of all mankind. It was, however, a life that had been purified and made new by love. And that is the life which is the New Life and which shall endure unto eternity.

Religious literature abounds in texts which celebrate the suffering of the Saviour. Similarly, there are many so-called 'spiritualities of the cross', some of which give rise to attitudes and deeds which may be generous and sincere but which are, none the less, often unhealthy. We used to offer to man the ideal of the resigned Christian whose back was bent to receive lashes from the whip of fate. And man rebelled. He turned away from us—although we Christians are the only ones who can save man from despair in the face of suffering and death.

It is not the blood shed by Jesus which saves the world. It is not suffering that redeems. Only love redeems. Suffering is an evil, even after the Redemption. When the Church says, 'O happy fault because of which we have been given a Saviour', she is not canonising sin. Because Jesus made

use of suffering as the occasion for redeeming us, we must
not be tempted to attribute some magical power to it. We
must not 'resign ourselves' to suffering and seek it out.
Jesus did not look for suffering and death. He did not save
man by committing suicide. Instead, in the midst of the
Event which was his life on earth, he lived suffering. He
was arrested, tried, condemned, tortured, and executed.
All these things happened to him in human history, just as
they have happened to other men before and after him. He
did not try to escape from them as though he were some
sort of wonder-working demigod rather than the Man-
God who is Love. He submitted. He did not refuse to
accept a single instant of it. What was forced upon him
from without, he accepted within himself. When his
executioners thought they had taken his life by force, he,
in a gesture of infinite love, took it and gave it willingly.
He used what happened to him. He joined together in it
all the suffering and death and all the 'passions' of his
brothers who fight for the development of mankind and the
world. He made up for the monstrous and senseless suffering which is the result of sin. And, having taken upon
himself the intolerable weight of all this, he caused it to
become, through love, an acceptable exchange for sin.
Thus, out of suffering and death he forged the material of
redemption. From infinite love, which is the conqueror of
non-love, he worked the Redemption.

Suffering in itself is worth nothing. Only love can give
life.

The Redemption was carried out to its completion. All
men have been saved, and the whole of creation has been
re-established in love. But Jesus does not want to save man
if man is unknowing or unwilling. He does not wish it,
because if he did save man in that way he would have to do

violence to man's freedom and, therefore, to man's dignity: 'All of us who possess the first-fruits of the Spirit, we too groan inwardly as we wait for our bodies to be set free. For we must be content to hope that we shall be saved' (*Rom.* 8:23). Man must not only receive and accept salvation from the hands of Christ; he must also participate. Otherwise, God would be a paternalistic God—the kind of God that, as we have already said, cannot be God. 'And if we are children [of God] we are heirs as well: heirs of God and coheirs with Christ, sharing his sufferings so as to share his glory' (*Rom.* 8:17). But Jesus goes even further. Just as we are responsible for the realisation of creation, so too are we responsible for the actualisation of the Redemption. It is up to us to being salvation to mankind and to the universe.

And so, the Redemption, which has been lived by Jesus, the Head of the body of humanity, must now be realised, day by day, in the members of that body. But just as the mystery of the Creation and of the Incarnation of Jesus Christ can be complete only with man's free assent, the mystery of the Redemption can become effective only through the full and loving consent of each one of us: 'In my own body [I] do what I can to make up all that has still to be undergone by Christ for the sake of his body, the Church' (*Col.* 1:24). What is missing from the sufferings of Christ is not human suffering; he has already accepted, borne, and offered human suffering to the Father. What is missing is that we freely give him our suffering, and that, in him and with him, we offer our suffering for the salvation of the world.

We Christians, therefore, must not make a mere pious memory of Christ's passion. The 'way of the Cross' is not a spiritual exercise suitable for those tender souls who are more concerned with the past than with the present and the future. The true Way of the Cross is not finished, for it has two dimensions. In one dimension, it was completed by Jesus Christ two thousand years ago, in the streets of Jerusalem. In the second dimension, however, the Way of the Cross is being followed by the whole of humanity, by all the members of Jesus Christ. This Way of the Cross comprises all the streets of humanity, all the paths of history and of time. It runs through man's torn body, through his divided heart, through his convulsed being. It passes through divided couples, destroyed families. It passes through the world of labour, and through the organisation or disorganisation of labour by which man is made a slave. It passes through the lines of the unemployed, through understaffed and inadequate schools, through slums, hospitals, prisons. It passes through under-developed countries. It passes through the battlefields. It passes everywhere that there is suffering, great or small, since all suffering affects man and strikes at the total body of humanity.

The cross dominates the world and time as it dominated Jerusalem. For sin too remains and unfolds in time, just as the Redemption is a divine and continuing action—an uninterrupted mystery of love which shall last as long as the race of man.

How can man, free and loving, enter into the heart of this mystery and live it as a conqueror with Jesus Christ the Conqueror?

The first battle to be fought is that against sin. It is, however, a battle that we cannot hope to win by ourselves. We need Christ. God was unable to leave us alone to face our non-love, to harm ourselves or others, to kill one another like unnatural brothers in a family feud. He therefore sent his Son, not to force us to cease sinning (for that would violate our human freedom), but to deliver us from our sin by taking it upon himself and obtaining forgiveness for it. If we renew that redemptive act with Jesus Christ and in him, then we will save ourselves and our brothers.

Today, man must consciously give to Christ the sins for which Christ has already made himself responsible. In order to do this, man must first recognise his sins and admit that he has committed them. He must also recognise and acknowledge the collective sins of social classes and communities, from the very smallest to the largest (which is humanity itself), in which man lives out his life. No man today can 'wash his hands'. No man can say that he is not responsible for those terrible plagues which are the collective sins of humanity. These sins surround us on all sides. They take place before our very eyes. They cause all mankind to cry out in pain; and in those cries we hear a question which God asked long ago: 'What have you done to your brother?'

Today's Christian, if he is mature, will rise above the narrow concept of his own little sins, his violations of a set of regulations that was composed for children. Instead, he must examine his whole life in order to discover the acts of non-love—his own, and those for which he bears the responsibility along with his associates.

Once more we see the fundamental necessity for a Christian to live his life fully. If he is able to face up to the reality of his daily life, in the circumstances in which the Father has placed him, then he will be able to uncover, acknowledge, and take upon himself his own sins and his share of the sins of the world. The more fully he lives his life in those human societies into which he was born, the more he will be consciously 'committed' to his world, and the more he will become a true brother to those around him. He will become 'one of them'; or rather, he will become them by sharing their joys, their suffering, their victories, and their defeats. In short, the more 'incarnated' a man is, the more easily will he be able to detect, accept, and bear his sin and the sin of his brothers.

Once more let us say that Jesus Christ waits for man in the midst of daily life and in all the dimensions of that life. Since Christ's passion, man can no longer despair, no matter what his sin or that of his brothers. He is no longer alone with that sin; for Christ the Redeemer is mysteriously there, waiting silently for man's free response to his saving love. That response must be an essential act of faith: 'Jesus, I believe that your love is stronger than my sin and that of my brothers. I believe that no sin exists which you have not already taken upon yourself. I believe that forgiveness has already been granted, for your conquering love has destroyed evil as fire consumes wood. Today, I freely give my sin, and that of my world, to you; and with you and in you, I give it to the Father, so that I may consciously receive from your hands a new life, that life of pure love which, on Calvary, you restored to all of mankind.'

The Christian must live that spiritual attitude every day of his life. But he must also make it effective through use of the sacrament of penance. In this way, the Redemption is reintroduced into time, into the life of man and the life of the world.

The Redemption as we have seen is not only a struggle and a victory over sin. It is also a struggle and a victory over suffering and death—over that suffering and death that Jesus Christ grasped, took to himself, and 'dynamised' by means of his infinite love. Nothing that we have said about acknowledging our sins and giving them to the Father, in Christ the Saviour, would be valid if we were not willing to participate also in the struggle which is the second aspect of the unique act of our salvation.

Before thinking of accepting and offering suffering to God, the Christian must fight against suffering. That is an absolute obligation. Otherwise, the Christian becomes that 'resigned soul' whose attitude is entirely contrary to man's God-given and essential dignity. We cannot repeat often enough that suffering is an evil, and that we must do all we can to control it and reduce it. That effort is one of the aspects of man's involvement in creation: the painful and tragic confrontation and struggle between an intelligent creature and the universe which he gradually conquers and dominates; the individual and collective struggle ranging from direct action on raw material and on life to action in a world and a human race already transformed. This, in a word, is the function of work, of technology, of all the sciences. It involves a commitment to man's political, social, and economic structures, and not only commitment but also participation. It requires that man be actively present in the battle to develop and complete the world— a battle in which all men are related to one another, in which those who suffer and die are soldiers killed in action, and in which progress is achieved only at the price of temporary defeat, of wounds and pain. All of this, and this alone, allows mankind to go forward.

If man is to become more human, and if the Christian is to become more a child of God, he will not do so by being passive in the face of suffering, but by fighting against suffering. The blood shed for the mastery of the universe, for the establishment of a just society, for the liberation of man and his integral development, is a redemptive force. Thus, a sick man, before offering his suffering to God, must fight with all his strength against his sickness. The labourer must fight against the pain of work, and also against inhuman working conditions. The student must struggle with the difficulty of overcoming the world by knowledge; but he must also fight against the abnormal conditions imposed on man 'in order to train his mind'. In other words, man must fight against all suffering —against both the suffering which man experiences in trying to master the world, and the suffering which results from his own selfishness, which is a supernumerary suffering that is caused by all of man's individual and collective sins.

If we can never resign ourselves to suffering, if we can never give up the struggle against it, and if we can (and sometimes we can indeed) decrease suffering, we must admit that suffering is, in one sense, invincible. For one thing, the struggle against suffering itself causes suffering. And that is the mystery. And that is the signal for rebellion and despair among those who do not know, or do not believe that, since Jesus' passion, there is an extraordinary force concealed within suffering which is capable of raising up the world. That force is the strength of the Redemption. It is the infinite strength of Jesus' redemptive love. It is the unitive strength of man burdened with sin and of the body of humanity which develops in history and in the world. It is the strength of a world perpetually harassed by a destructive non-love. It is the living strength which is ever victorious over death.

This strength, however, is a hidden force. It can be perceived only by the eyes of a believer. It is also a captive force, which only man's freedom can take and set free so that it may become operative. To take advantage of that strength, man has only to go to Jesus Christ, the Redeemer, who waits for him in the midst of suffering. For before that suffering belonged to man, it belonged to the Saviour. Jesus took it, lived it, and made it part of himself. He entered into it, transformed it, and dynamised it with all the power of his love by reclaiming it in order to give it to the Father, as a free gift.

We have said that, even at the purely human level, man can grow through suffering if, instead of resigning himself to it, he struggles against it and integrates it into his upward climb. For the believer, however, suffering can also be the occasion for his own salvation and that of the world; he has only to consent to meet the suffering and triumphant Christ in the midst of each one of his sufferings, and to refuse to live life only on its surface.

Man was given the Redemption before he could freely take it to himself. Now, he must, while living, take it from the hands of Jesus Christ—not in a sort of mystical rapture or through imaginary sufferings, but by being totally present in his everyday life. It is there, and nowhere else, that man will find his path in the unique and true Way of the Cross which leads to the resurrection.

The energy of which we have spoken, which lies at the heart of suffering, is too often forgotten; and man too often deprives himself of his greatest means of liberation, renewal, unity, and progress. Man wants to save himself alone and to build the world without setting free the love won by Jesus Christ, the love which is mysteriously available within the smallest suffering. But man cannot reformulate the economy of salvation in time. If the mortar of love is not present around every stone of his edifice, he builds in vain. Since the advent of sin into the world, that love can flourish only as the result of a painful but victorious effort by the suffering members of Christ. We must not waste a single human suffering, or the Redemption cannot be fully realised for the men of our time.

Often, too, the strength hidden in suffering is misused. We make use of suffering for itself, and ignore its redemptive content. Too often man decides to 'go it alone' with his misfortune, to remain crushed under the weight of injustices and of sufferings which someone has advised him to 'offer up for the salvation of your soul'. And that is one of the worst possible spiritual perversions. There is no question of allowing man to suffer, for suffering is an evil. What we must give man, beyond a suffering against which he has fought, is a meeting with the suffering Christ. We must never thank God for suffering, any more than we can thank him for sin. But we should thank him for allowing us to meet the Saviour, who, despite sin and despite suffering, waits for us to allow us to benefit from his struggle and his victory *against* sin and suffering.

It is not true that 'God tries those whom he loves'. But it is true that the more we suffer, the more Christ is present in us. Because he has already suffered and conquered our suffering, he is aware of us and available to us—not to remove our suffering, but to allow us to conquer it in turn, through his love, and to turn it into a redemptive force.

As long as a child plays quietly, his mother remains in the kitchen preparing dinner. But if he does something naughty and hurts himself, his screams will bring the mother running to help him. Despite his behaviour, she is there, more attentive and loving than ever. But the child, none the less, can rebel against his hurt. He can throw himself on the floor; he can kick the piece of furniture on which he hurt himself; he can strike out at his mother who is trying to help him. In that case, he suffers even more, for his pain remains and he now has to bear it alone—along with his frustration. But if he loves his mother, he goes beyond his pain and throws himself into her arms. She does not take away the hurt, but, in holding her child, she bears his hurt with him.

In the same way, suffering can either separate us from God or bring us closer to him. Man can reject Jesus, who is present within that suffering. He can accuse Jesus of causing the pain and try to 'get even' with Jesus. Or, having heard Jesus softly speak his invitation to love, he can, by assenting with all his strength to Jesus' redemptive act, abandon himself to the Saviour, and offer himself by allowing himself to be offered. In that sense, where there is much sin, there Jesus is most present in order to receive and pardon. Where there is much suffering, Jesus is most present in order to save his child; that is, to love him.

Mary accompanied Jesus on the Way of the Cross. She stood near him on Calvary. But she was not beaten with Jesus, and she was not crucified with him. And yet, the Church calls her the 'co-Redemptrice'—the redeemer-with-Christ. The reason is that she silently united herself to all the suffering of her son—just as the mother did in the preceding example. She bore his suffering, and she offered it to God with him. She was powerless to stop the torture of her son; but she was all-powerful when it came to redeeming the world with her son. It was a miracle of love.

We have all, at one time or another, been crushed by, and rebelled against, the suffering of another. What doctor or nurse has not felt the frustration of being powerless in the face of approaching death? What man, engaged in the struggle against injustice in his own community or in the world, has not felt the temptation to despair because of the apparent futility of his efforts? We are men of little faith; and we have wasted valuable time because of it. Instead, we should make use of all of our redemptive power. This does not mean that we should regard it as some sort of magical panacea to be hauled out once all human resources have been exhausted. It means, rather, that at the moment of greatest discouragement we discover, within suffering but going infinitely beyond it, a treasure by virtue of which we are enabled to accept life just when we thought we were about to be overcome by death.

What we lack today are contemplatives in the midst of life, men who, while fighting in the thick of the battle against suffering, are able to withdraw to the foot of the world's cross. We lack militants of pure love to appear before the unknown or rejected love, communicants with Christ the Redeemer. Without such men, all the suffering of man and humanity will be to no avail.

In the face of our suffering brothers, in the sight of tortured humanity, we are invited to share the co-redemption of Mary, who stands powerless but all-powerful at the foot of the cross.

We have said several times that it is wrong to seek out suffering for its own sake; it is even a sickness. We do not willingly make ourselves suffer just to prove our love for someone. There are saints who have inflicted suffering on themselves. That is no surprise, any more than it is a surprise that, centuries ago, lovers used to risk their lives in tournaments for the sake of their ladies. Today, however, there are other ways for lovers to prove their love; there are studies to be undertaken, professions to be prepared for, a commitment to society to be worked out. These things involve much in the way of sacrifice and suffering. And the same holds true for Christians. If we are sometimes asked to make a sacrifice—during Lent, for example—it is not in order to create suffering so that we may be able to 'offer it up'. Its purpose is to make possible a real step forward, to allow us to develop a fuller life that we may offer to God. What we must do, in effect, is to make a choice: we must deprive ourselves of something in order to get something better. We prune roses in order to produce more beautiful roses. And we must prune our lives—not so that we may die, but so that we may live more fully. We must choose life. And to choose life is to choose the development of life. The kingdom of the Father is not built on ruins.

Thus, we should not attempt to bypass the sufferings that come to us in the ordinary course of life and invent new ones of our own manufacture. We must accept our limitations—those of our bodies, our minds, our acts, our lives, our commitment to life—as dictated by such persons and events as constitute the circumstances of our lives. We must accept such limitations in order to create the world which the Father desires, and we must take the weight of our suffering as an indication of the extent of our life-giving activity. The man who sits by the side of the road and refuses to get involved in life will not suffer—unless perhaps he deliberately chooses to sit on sharp rocks, in order to create some suffering for himself. Such suffering cannot be reclaimed. Jesus has not taken it within himself. He is not present in it.

Where man truly suffers and dies is in the accomplishment of his human tasks. And he dies a real death; for we spend our lives in dying so that we may live more fully. The man who wants to save his life will lose it. Only the man who is willing to accept the life of each day as a free gift will grow. This gift of life is the gift of oneself to others and for the sake of others. It is made directly in interpersonal relationships; and indirectly through the intermediary of familiar, social, economic, and political institutions. When we join a union, a community association, a club, or a movement, what we are doing is joining ourselves to others and giving ourselves to others.

Man, however, cannot give himself unless he renounces himself, unless he dies to himself. To express it concretely, I cannot both smoke a cigarette and give it to a friend. I cannot put on my slippers and settle down for a night of television and, at the same time, attend a union meeting. I cannot talk and, at the same time, listen. I cannot concentrate on obtaining what I want for myself and, at the same time, work for others.

Man is prone to be self-centred. We make little gods of ourselves. That is not necessarily wrong; for we must indeed become gods—but we must do so with God and by God, through Jesus Christ, who became man so that we might become gods. Our whole lives must be a sustained effort to forget ourselves so that we may think, in Jesus Christ, of other men and of the world which is to be built. That is the essential sacrifice. That is the true 'spirituality' of daily life: to die to ourselves so that we may have life more abundantly. It is a painful but exhilarating and perpetual process of being born anew.

Jesus Christ was the first to commit himself to suffering and death through love of life; and his commitment involved the taking upon himself of all the sufferings and all the deaths of all men in the past and the future. The Christian, in his turn, must now freely embark with Jesus on that unique and total Passion in his daily life. If the Christian dies to himself every day, he will attain life—true life, which is the life of man; an expanded, transfigured, divinised, and eternal life.

At the end of our life on earth, when we die the final death of a series of deaths, we will have the most beautiful and complete opportunity to live, in Jesus Christ, the mystery of the Redemption. This final death to ourselves by the process of biological dissolution is the final stage in our development, the final step in our climb toward transfiguration, the ultimate liberation from our limitations so that we may emerge into life. It is a blessing for man to be able consciously to experience that dissolution, to be able

willingly to offer the gift of his final breath to the Father
with Jesus and in him, for the salvation of the world.

Jesus Christ, then, has willed to need man to live the
mystery of the Redemption—just as he needs him to live
the mysteries of Creation and the Incarnation—to reintrod-
uce it into time, first of all by acknowledging his sins and
those of his world, and then by offering those sins consciously to the Father through Jesus Christ. He does so
also by fighting with all his strength against suffering, and
by freeing the energy which is hidden within suffering
through communion with the Redeemer. And finally, he
does so by accepting and living with Jesus Christ all of his
deaths-to-himself, even to the final and ultimate death.
Man must make a daily and loving response to the freely
given love of the Saviour. In this way, man is saved and
himself becomes a saviour with Christ—no longer, as St
Paul says, 'in hope', but in fact; and all of mankind and the
universe itself then enter into that life which is Eternal
Life.

The mystery of the Redemption is also the mystery of the
Resurrection; for the Way of the Cross does not end at
the tomb, but continues beyond death and leads to the
joy of life eternal. Jesus Christ is the great conqueror of
sin, suffering, and death. In him, every man, and all of
mankind—past, present, and future—are dead and brought
to life again: God 'brought us to life with Christ—it is
through grace that you have been saved—and raised us up
with him and gave us a place with him in heaven, in Christ
Jesus' (*Eph.* 2:5–6). And so, there is no one, no sin, not a
moment of our lives, not a particle of the universe, which
is not affected by Christ's victory. Nothing is outside the
Redemption which has been accomplished. He has
gathered all things within himself: man, humanity, the

world. He has offered all things, given all things, made all things 'happen' in God; and all things have been restored to life.

If we are willing, every moment of our lives can resound with the joy of Easter. And the true Christian cannot live without joy. Through Christ, he encounters joy and lives in joy. He is given over to joy. In his life there can be no enduring failure—neither suffering nor death are insurmountable obstacles for him. Everything is the raw material of redemption, of resurrection, for, in the middle of his sufferings and his deaths, Christ the Conqueror waits. If a Christian is unhappy, it can only be because he has succumbed to the temptation to flirt with death and to turn his back on life. For that reason, the greatest suffering and the greatest joy can coexist in the same life and be intimately interconnected. By 'joy' we do not mean the transient (though legitimate) pleasure that comes from comfort, or the false happiness of the simple mind that is unaware of his degradation, or the 'virtuous' resignation of a pseudo-mystic, or the blind optimism of the man who figures that 'it is better to laugh than to cry'. We mean rather the calm, the interior serenity, and the profound peace which permeate and emanate from a man who, notwithstanding a torn heart and body, and despite the suffering of mankind and the world, believes with all his strength in the victory of the Saviour. And he believes this without for an instant forgetting or denying the existence of suffering and sin, and without giving up the fight against them.

The man who has entered into this joy and remains in it becomes, in Christ, what the Father wants him to be. He has reached his true level, as a man who is totally developed; for he has reached the ultimate stage in his communion with the Mystery of Jesus—not only the mystery of Creation; not only the mystery of Incarnation; not only the mystery of Redemption. But also the mystery of *Resurrection*.

PART III

PART III

8. The Encounter with God

We firmly believe that modern man and the modern world, without being conscious of it, are calling to God with all their strength. That call is often a silent one, from the subconscious of individuals or from that of mankind collectively. But sometimes it is the desperate cry of men victimised and crushed by our great 'consumer society'—of men who are supposed to be the beneficiaries, but become the slaves, of that society. That cry comes principally from the young, who, before they can be anaesthetised and smothered by the urge to 'have', scream out their hunger to 'be'. Often, they have no idea of what it is they want to be or what they should be. Their rebellion is a revolt, which takes place in the most complete disorder, against everything that appears to limit man in his body, his mind, his love, and in the desire to surpass himself by attaining a degree of development and expansion as yet undreamed of. It is also an expression of the eternal quest for total love —but outside of love's so-called middle-class frame of reference, which is said to be too restrictive. Thus, these young people demand, and often live, sexual freedom. They are looking for a love to satisfy their famished bodies, but without taking into account that their hunger comes from beyond the body. It is a hunger of the soul, and it rises above the body through which it is felt. Thus, they attempt to penetrate into 'another world' by means of drugs and esoteric cults; or they simply try to establish a new life-style by cultivating 'originality' and experimenting in human relationships—hence the phenomena of the hippies, beatniks, and so forth. All of this, very likely, is founded in discouragement and disillusionment with realistic efforts to build a new society; but it also reflects a will to question values deeply at a time when, in the face of so many failures, the desire and the vision of a beautiful future is growing.

All of these things are indications of aspirations and ideals rooted in the heart of man—aspirations to truth, to justice, to responsibility, to unity, to harmony, to peace on earth—aspirations ever present, but never satisfied. And this holds true now, in particular, when man stands astonished by his own knowledge and power, and trembling before the possibilities that are opening up.

Men today—especially men who no longer need to struggle continually in order to live—are finding that they are disoriented, and sometimes anguished, when they reflect on their own lives and on that of the world. It used to be that only poets and philosophers asked the questions that entire groups of people ask today: Why are we alive? Where does life come from? Where does it lead? Who are we?

And when men have the opportunity to avoid being stifled by a superabundance of material goods, or hypnotised by the uncontrolled desire for them, they sense, or realise, that the possession of such goods—useful and legitimate as they may be in themselves—does not satisfy them. They then try somehow to rise above them, to become better, to build a world that is more solid and durable. They look for 'something better'—for a real reason 'to be' and 'to be more fully'.

I think that the present crisis, with its revolts, its searching, its suffering, is the first contraction in the birth of a new world. Mankind is becoming more aware, and this awareness involves a great responsibility, a great opportunity for man today. Mature men are beginning to see the light at the end of the tunnel—and their first reaction is a cry of anguish. They are looking for their beginning and their end. They are looking for their Father.

Why, then, are there some Christians who are afraid? At every new birth of his creatures, God is present. We have said, and we may repeat, that in all of man's aspirations, in all of his intolerable suffering, in all of his absences, in all of his anguish, God is there, inviting man to discover that there is something beyond man, beyond history, beyond the universe. The heart and body of man may be tormented; but in his mind there is a sign of his divine origin which points out to him the long road to the very source of his being. There are the sounds of a Creator-Love which come to him from beyond time and suggest to him the possibility of his full development and his divinisation in Jesus Christ. Man cannot ignore that suggestion without denying his own nature, for he was created to become a son of God; God 'chose us, chose us in Christ . . . determining that we should become his adopted sons, through Jesus Christ' (*Eph.* 1:4–5).

We believe with all our strength that God today is calling man; and that man, blind and surrounded by darkness, is casting about, often unconsciously, to see where that voice is coming from.

Many of our contemporaries recognise the need for a radical change. They want, in fact, to create a 'new man' and a 'new world'. Some of them think, rather naïvely, that this new man will appear on his own, at the end of some natural process. Others are convinced that he will spring up once we have disposed of all the 'alienations' that now impede man's progress. Still others say that the new man will be the result of a new society, in which all present social, political, and economic structures will be overturned. But more and more men of all persuasions are beginning to be apprehensive because they see no indication that the new man is about to appear. They are beginning to sense their own powerlessness. And, in fact, even though technology and science are making giant strides forward, man is remaining pretty much what he has always been. It is true that, despite serious failures and unforgivable delays, there have been certain cultural improvements and a certain influx of material goods into some segments of society which hitherto were almost totally deprived. But the beneficiaries of these improvements are still themselves. They are eager to possess more, but not concerned about *being* more. In some countries in which this process of material amelioration has taken place, the older generation is astonished that their children, who were born within these new structures, are no different from themselves.

In the same way, we are discovering every day, through modern methods of communication, that man is essentially the same everywhere, in all countries, under all political or economic or social regimes, at every level of development. And so vanishes our hope that man, by an increase in knowledge and in goods and in material power over himself and over life, might improve morally and attain the state of being 'more'. The contrary, in fact, seems to be the case. As man grows richer in earthly things, he seems more and more threatened. The forces within man—those of his mind and his heart and his life—seem less under control than ever before, less unified, less balanced. Many of us are like hand grenades from which the pins have been removed; sooner or later, we are going to explode all over our lives. Men no longer seem capable of mastering themselves. They no longer have the strength to 'build themselves', or the will to do so. And what is worse, they do not know where to find the source of energy that is necessary to effect a synthesis. They do not even know what the plan of construction is.

As we develop the will to create a radically new man and a radically new world, there develops, along with it, confusion as to what kind of man and world to build. Some men are beginning to grasp, however tenuously, that man must be transformed and changed far more than they had originally thought; that man needs a permanent revolution *in his heart*, the necessity for which no other kind of revolution can obviate. And then, these men pin their hopes to whatever hero happens to be in vogue at the moment in the world of the intellect or in that of action. They expect these 'stars' to furnish on request a doctrine, an ideal, and a mysterious 'power' that will be able to change man. But none of these men are the latter-day saviours that are needed and expected.

Christ is still shut up in the churches, they say, and that is why some men are unwilling to call on him and why others do not even think of turning toward him. They say that Christ is the private property of medieval ghosts who wear cassocks or wimples. They say that he is a personage dreamed up to satisfy children eager for miracles, to awaken enthusiasm in adolescents, to console the aged, the sick, and single ladies of pious inclination. They may even think that Jesus was a remarkable man, that his ideas and his ideals—although a bit mysterious and utopian—are beautiful; but they say, in the next breath, that Jesus' teachings have been betrayed by his followers, and that he is as dead as the founders of other movements.

We, however, believe that it is the living Christ whom many of our contemporaries seek unconsciously. It is the saving Christ whom they expect to build a new man and a new world—a man and a world more beautiful, greater, and more exciting than they could ever imagine. Man alone can never find the means to save himself; and, if he looks for them at ground level, he will be wasting his time. We believe what revelation tells us: 'This is the stone rejected by you the builders, but which has proved to be the keystone. For of all the names in the world given to men, this is the only one by which we can be saved' (*Acts* 4:11–12). We learn the same thing from the experience of failure—and it is the Holy Spirit who speaks through that experience, and who invites us. We firmly believe—though many deny it—that now is the time of Christ, and that we must now proclaim and reveal him as the true Christ, Man-God, living and triumphant. We must show that he is not a caricature, and not a corpse.

Our contemporaries will discover Christ in his overwhelming truth only if we, as Christians, have truly encountered him ourselves.

Man is looking for God. Man needs God. But who can encounter God? No one. Jesus himself said it: 'No one has ever seen God'. But then Jesus added: 'It is the only Son, who is nearest to the Father's heart, who has made him known' (*John* 1:18).

And that is it. There is no other way to see God, to know him, to unite oneself to him, other than in Jesus Christ. And Jesus repeated this idea many times. He said that he was *the* way, *the* truth, *the* life; that no one went to the Father except through him; that whoever saw him saw the Father; that the Father was in him and he was in the Father. Jesus came to save the world, and except in him there can be no salvation for man: 'God loved the world so much that he gave his only Son, so that everyone who believes in him may not be lost but may have eternal life. For God sent his Son into the world not to condemn the world, but so that through him the world might be saved' (*John* 3:16–17). And

then St John says (1:11–12), 'He came to his own domain
. . . to all who did accept him he gave power to become children of God'. There is no need to go on; one could quote
the entire Gospel to prove this point. It is simply a matter of
this: we must believe in the central Event in history, the
Incarnation of God; we must truly believe in Jesus Christ,
God, who came among men to save man and the world; we
must believe that in Jesus there is the power necessary to
touch the heart of man and transform him completely; we
must believe that the mystery of Jesus Christ is unfolding
in time, and that our God is present, in us, with us, among
us, living with our life, conquering, until the end of time.

The crucial question in all this is that of our relationship
with Christ. The man who separates himself from Christ,
who loses sight of him, separates himself from God and
turns his back on salvation—that is, he turns his back on
the opportunity for his own full development and the
building of a better world. *The man who loses Jesus loses
everything.*

In the contemporary Church there are constant meetings
and conferences, composed of bishops, priests, religious,
and laymen, the purpose of which is to study, discuss, and
research the best means of evangelising modern man. There
are sessions, innumerable committees, staff personnel, and
new structures constantly being created. There are innova-
tors offering new ideas, techniques, and revolutionary
methods. There are conservatives trying to apply the
brakes, and there are militants defending the cause of
'progress' and change. This is all very well. It is even
necessary. But we must ask ourselves what the source is of
all this activity. Is it a more intimate contact with Christ,
which is itself the result of more frequent and extended
contacts? Is it primarily not the defence of methods, or

research, or organisation and structures, or ideas and even dogma, rather than a great love, a 'passion' for someone— for Jesus Christ as contemplated in his mystical and historical dimensions? Are our most militant revolutionaries and our most steadfast contestants those who are most intimate with and most enthusiastic for Christ? For that must be the criterion against which we measure the authenticity of their work. 'Make sure that no one traps you and deprives you of your freedom by some secondhand, empty, rational philosophy based on the principles of this world instead of on Christ. In his body lives the fullness of divinity' (*Col.* 2:8–9).

Among all those people who gather to study and decide 'priorities', to organise the preaching of Christ—for everyone says that that is what it is all about—how many are there who do, in fact, preach Christ? And how much time is there left for them to get started on that all-important work?

Is there anyone left who preaches Christ instead of discussing the methodology of preaching Christ? Is there anyone left among us who, because he has met Christ and lives with him and has daily been transformed by him in the Gospel and in life, can preach his discovery, his certitude, his love, instead of mumbling words that are full of excuses?

The desire to change and progress within the Church is indeed praiseworthy. But we are running the risk of ignoring the only thing that is essential. In our desire to make improvements, it is not impossible that we are smothering the *spirit* of Christ under a fabric woven of our subtle thoughts, our organisations, tactics, and techniques. It is possible that, as we sit weaving our splendid plans for the future, our contemporaries are dying of hunger in their search for a living Person, a Saviour.

Jesus Christ, we have said, is the Son of God who came among men two thousand years ago. But he is also the 'Great Christ' who has incorporated all mankind into his love and made 'members' of all men. He is the Mystery of Christ, the mystery of Creation, of Incarnation, of Redemption and Resurrection, and he is not limited to thirty years of human history. He covers and embodies the entire history of the human race.

This is the 'total Christ', in his dual dimension: the historical Jesus and the Risen Christ, who lives in his members and in the world. This is the Christ whom we must encounter if we are not to lose our spiritual balance and if we do not wish our witness to be in vain.

We have said that there have been Christians, especially in the past, who knew the historical Jesus. They prayed to the historical Jesus, contemplated him, and tried to imitate him. But Jesus, despite all this, remained outside their lives and external to them. He was merely a model whom those Christians admired and whose life-style they tried to duplicate. That style was soon translated into religious rituals, which then came often to be regarded as magical means to attain eternal life.

It seems that this sort of spirituality was only a 'phase', a stage of development which corresponds roughly to a spiritual adolescence. Carried to an extreme, it can produce a real separation between life and faith and leave whole sectors of human life—particularly life in society—without the influence of Jesus.

We have seen (and suffered from) too many of these Christians who 'practise' a 'religion' which has nothing to do with life. We have come to realise that we cannot know Christ unless we know all the members of his Body. We cannot love him unless we love all his brothers and unless we participate with him, in our lives, in all the aspects of his Mystery.

To accept Christ, the Head, without accepting all of his members and his total Mystery, is to mutilate Christ.

It will be one of the glories of our generation of Christians to have rediscovered concretely the 'mystical dimension' of Jesus Christ, to have realised that we can actually discover the living Christ in our brother men and in all the events of our lives and the life of the world.

That is the difficult, demanding, but exhilarating task of a mature faith, which gives meaning to life and to the world and which makes of us, at each instant, Christ's collaborators in realising the plan of the Father.

The problem, however, is that the dangers and the possible errors implicit in that discovery are proportionately great. Christians today are passionately involved in building up the world; and they risk forgetting what lies beyond that constructive process; or they risk the temptation to postpone until later what must be lived here and now, because it is an interior reality. We are not building a spaceship, which must be constructed from the ground up, with the capsule itself coming last in the order of execution. To believe that we are doing something analogous to that can lead to a new and even more obvious separation between the life of man and the world and 'Christian' life.

Another danger is that the Christian, fascinated by the discovery of Christ living in men and in history, may neglect the historical Jesus Christ and may neglect to meditate on his life. If we forget the Jesus of history, then it becomes impossible for us to find him in life. If we arrange to meet someone at a crowded railway station, and we have never seen that person before, how can we pick him out of a crowd of people milling about? In the same way, a man who has never 'seen' the Jesus of history cannot recognise him, cannot approach him or contemplate him. He is risking living a life of illusion—until the day he realises that, by definition, an illusion is unreal; that an illusion is a thing, or a person, that does not exist. And then he will say, 'I've lost my faith'. It would be more accurate to say, 'I've lost sight of Christ. I don't see him any more'.

In such cases, we may say that Christ is 'decapitated'. But where we decapitate Christ or mutilate him, the result is the same: we condemn ourselves to live without him. We have witnessed that phenomenon among Christians who, at one time or another of their lives and by one method or another, reach that state. They are deprived of animation, like corpses. For anyone who can no longer live through Christ condemns himself to death and his action becomes fruitless. 'Make your home in me', Jesus said (*John* 15:4–5), 'as I make mine in you. As a branch cannot bear fruit all by itself, but must remain part of the vine, neither can you unless you remain in me. . . . Whoever remains in me, with me in him, bears fruit in plenty; for cut off from me you can do nothing'.

If man is to make something of himself and the world, he must encounter Christ—but the *whole* Christ.

Must we first of all meet the historical Jesus, and then, knowing him, live with him and through him? Or must we first discover him among men, work with him, and then go and find him in the Gospel? Some people ask these questions. Some even accuse one another of having made the wrong choice, and, saying that the faith of this or that Christian has no value, they condemn one another without allowing any appeal.

There is no point in fighting about it. Jesus Christ, sent by the Father, arranges for man, individually or in groups, according to the needs of the time, to meet with him in love. But, through his Holy Spirit, he chooses different times and places for those meetings. We must respect his choice. Man has nothing to say about it; and neither have the theologians. All we can do is desire with all our strength to encounter the total Christ, so that we may have a life of faith that is solid and balanced. We must, however, allow for and respect the various ways in which different people attain that end. Throughout history, Jesus has revealed himself only gradually; and today too he shows himself only gradually to those who seek him out. The important fact is that we are invited to meet Jesus, to talk with him, to love him, so that we may be transformed and united in a common undertaking. It makes not the slightest difference how we receive that invitation and where we meet.

Let me say it once more: Why be afraid? What is the use of being afraid and thereby casting doubt on the validity of modern man's spiritual orientation?

For many decades we have admired men, both young and old, who have dedicated their lives to working for their fellow men, and especially for the poor. These men, working within the framework of their own lives, within their professions and their communities, have, in the course of their militant lives, discovered Jesus Christ. Some of them took a long time to recognise and identify Jesus; but those who witnessed their generous struggle for the poor, and their spiritual progress, have no doubt at all that Jesus was mysteriously present in them and in their work from the very beginning. One must entirely lack 'good faith' not to admit it, not to admire and be edified by the lives of certain 'militants' who burn with love for their brother men.

It disturbs some people to see these brilliant flowers blooming so profusely outside our carefully prepared gardens. And they ask, 'But do these people have *true* charity?' Certainly, we all know militants who are not 'devout' and even some who are not religious at all, at least at the beginning of their work. This is not surprising, and we should not be taken aback by it. We cannot cut love into pieces. There is only one love. And love expresses itself by forsaking oneself, forgetting oneself, for the sake of some-one else. Whenever anyone does this, he loves; and God is present in all real love. (See the first epistle of St John, chapter 4.)

Let the theologians discuss and study the nature of God's presence in love. That is what they are supposed to do. But they must abstain (and we should too) from issuing identity cards certifying that one is a Christian because one believes, or does, this or that. If the Gospel teaches us anything, it is that we must be very wary of well-established categories. Categories have nothing to do with love.

In this context, we must take into account the massive effect of almost fifty years of Catholic Action. We have only begun to realise the enormous riches that have come to the Church because of it. And to it we owe in large measure that marvellous 'experience' of the presence of the Risen Christ living among us, ready to reveal himself in the full light of day—but also sometimes in insupportable darkness —to all those who take part in serving their fellow men and in building up the world. We should thank the Holy Spirit, who has given such men to our time.

To sum up, we may say that we believe wholeheartedly that Jesus Christ is present to those men who are involved in life, that he reveals himself to them in the midst of their activities and invites them to a life of extraordinary union. But we believe too that these men must take into account Jesus' historical reality in order consciously to live the *total* Christ: '. . . so that Christ may live in your hearts through faith, and then, planted in love and built on love, you will with all the saints have strength to grasp the breadth and the length, the height and the depth; until knowing the love of Christ, which is beyond all knowledge, you are filled with the utter fullness of God' (*Eph.* 3:17–19).

9. 'I Am with You Always; Yes, to the End of Time'

Every life, and every moment of every life, is a moment of that 'sacred history' of the People of God who are visibly gathered together within the Church; of that history which began at the beginning of the world and which will endure until the end of time, until Jesus Christ, having gathered all things, all men, and all the universe unto himself, will offer all to the Father so that all may be transformed and transfigured in love.

Every event, no matter how insignificant, in the life of a man or a group of men is contained in the essential Event of history, which is the coming of God in Jesus Christ so that all things might be subjected to him. Every event, therefore, has an incalculable value because of its content— or rather, because of its 'interiority'. Every event is a moment of the Mystery of Christ which is taking place in time and to which nothing and no one is alien.

Man can live the Creation, the Incarnation, the Redemption, and the Resurrection in every one of his acts. He can live the Creation because by the very act of living he is completing his own creation and, in the company of his brothers, that of the world. He can live the Incarnation because, by accepting with love the presence of Jesus Christ, he allows Christ to take him over completely. He can live the Redemption since, because of sin, there is not a second of his life that does not necessitate struggle, suffering, and death to himself. If it is lived with Christ, that battle against selfishness, pride, and non-love can only lead to the victory of the Resurrection, by virtue of which that particle of life enters into Life—into true life, which is eternal.

Thus, the Christian who, through faith, discovers Christ living in the centre of life can join Christ and live out the Mystery of Christ with him. But he can also reject the encounter and union with Christ. He must therefore acquire the spiritual habit, as it were, of that encounter, through loyalty with respect to living his faith in his life. Just as he must go beyond the words of the Evangelists if he is to find Christ in the Gospel, so too must he go beyond life's events in order to find life itself.

Since all things are received into Christ, since everything is contained within the Event, it follows that all of life possesses a dimension which is invisible to bodily eyes, a certain mysterious 'inner dimension'.

This inner dimension is not something reserved for use after death. It is primarily a function of the here and now; for it is within every person, every event, every life.

If modern man and the modern world have trouble in believing in an inner dimension, it is because we have always presented it to them as divorced from the present, as 'another life' some time in the future which has no connection with this life. We have made Christians look up to heaven; and so they have lost interest in the earth. But there is no 'other life' which obliges us to ignore and despise the present life. There is indeed only one life, and that is the life that we are now living—a life which goes far beyond that which we experience through our senses, a life that our intellect alone cannot comprehend unless it is enlightened by faith. And that one, single life is the life which, at the end of our days on earth, will be profoundly transformed, transfigured, and restored in Christ, so that it may be lived out in eternity.

God is now present in the midst of that life. He has come down into life, permeated it, and given a supernatural dimension to it. He did not merely stitch one life, like a patch, to another, so that we might say, 'Well, this life ends here, and the next one begins there.' He added a dimension which gives life to all of life, just as the spirit gives life to the body.

God made the 'supernatural' come down to the 'natural', heaven to earth, in the most radical way possible. He sent his Son down to earth to live the life of a man, the Man-God: 'and the Word was made flesh'.

For a man to live an integral, total life, he must consciously relate within himself, within his brothers, within his life, within the life of the world, to that inner dimension. To live fully and intensively, in effect, is to live here and now—but the here and now in all its dimensions, in depth as well as in breadth. If life does not satisfy our needs, it is because we do not live life in its totality. When we are overcome with hunger for the infinite, for life, for love, truth, justice, and peace, it is not only a *future* life which motivates us, but also (and primarily) the need to live our present life perfectly, without limitations, as a life which has something about it of the infinite. What we want, in short, is heaven; but heaven here and now, rooted in the whole of our lives. And we are right in wanting it, for Christ has given it to us. He has given us *his* life, and, through it, the Kingdom which is now among us.

Christ said, 'I will be raised up so that I may draw all things to myself.' Then he entered into suffering and death. Finally, he emerged triumphant; he rose from the dead. Since that time, as Head of the human body, he draws to himself all of his members so that, in him, they may penetrate for all eternity into that inner dimension, into what lies beyond life today. That is, he draws all men to himself so that they may become the whole men that the Father wishes them to be.

Man has been created in God's image. But God is love, truth, justice, peace, etc. Therefore man has been created with a tendency toward love, truth, justice, peace, etc. This divine likeness in man should not be merely a blueprint. In and through Christ, it must become a reality. There is no human aspiration or ideal which is not, either clearly or obscurely, part of that likeness. That is, there is not one that is not an aspiration toward Christ, toward intimate union with him, so that in him may be constructed the man and the world that the Father has eternally desired.

This is true for man as an individual, and it is true for the various human communities, from the largest to the smallest, no matter whether they be social, labour, recreational, scholarly, or residential communities. God, in Jesus Christ, is equally present in the aspirations of all those groups. In fact, it is Christ who, in drawing them toward himself, inspires their search for liberty, dignity, justice, responsibility, pleasure, etc.

That is not to say that all the aspirations of man and of human groups are necessarily healthy ones. Many of them are often deformed, perverted from their true purpose, misappropriated by man for his own profit and advantage when man either does not know God or thinks that he can do without God. Such is the heritage of original sin. It is capable of diverting the course of human aspirations; but it is not capable of destroying those aspirations. For Jesus Christ is too strong to allow it. By his redemptive Incarnation, he has set what had been diverted on its proper path again. The man who struggles is therefore assured of victory—if only he struggles alongside the one who is the great Liberator.

If we believe in man's aspirations, in man's desire to better himself, to live more fully, to build a just and united world, then we believe in the Father who creates in love. And we believe in Jesus Christ, the Saviour. And we also believe in the Holy Spirit. For the Holy Spirit also came down to earth. Christ had promised to send him: 'I shall ask the Father, and he will give you another Advocate to be with you for ever, that Spirit of truth . . . you know him, because he is with you, he is in you' (*John* 14:15–17). And Christ kept his word.

The Holy Spirit is always with us. And the Scriptures tells us what his function is from all eternity. He was present at all of creation. He spoke through the prophets. He prepared Mary for the coming of the Saviour, and he 'overshadowed' her on the day of the Event.

Today, the Holy Spirit is still at work in the heart of man and of the world. He accompanies and guides man in the completion of creation. It is he who straightens what has been twisted. It is he who makes straight the way of the Saviour. He is present in all human aspirations, and he corrects in them what must be corrected. He directs them. He prepared the encounter between man and Christ within the framework of involvement in the realisation of what would otherwise remain merely a plan.

It is not enough for man to aspire to justice, liberty, peace, and fraternity. It is not enough to preach the necessity for the liberation of man, of the oppressed, and of the poor. We must commit ourselves to the realisation of those ideals. That is the work which is proper to man in the completion of creation according to the will of the Father, as we explained earlier in this book (see chapter 5). Man's initial response to his aspirations, which are really words of Christ spoken through his Holy Spirit, must be to become involved. It is by action (as St John tells us in his first epistle), and not solely by words, that man must love his brothers. By action in the service of mankind, man begins to realise, concretely and historically, the Mystery of Christ. And the Mystery of Christ itself is thereby 'activated' within the Father's eternal plan of love for man and the world. For that plan is not purely 'spiritual'; it involves the work of creation, and also the taking of that creation unto himself by Christ the Saviour.

Man's aspirations and ideals are the same throughout the world, although they are felt, expressed, and lived in different ways according to man's varying situation. They exist in the heart of every man, regardless of race, class, age, philosophy, or religion—and also regardless of the notion that man has of them. They all have the same source, for all men are called to be sons of God and to participate in building the Body of Christ. In this way, a non-believer who takes these aspirations seriously, who rises above himself and works for the betterment of mankind and the world, also works within the plan of the Father, with Jesus Christ and in Jesus Christ. And this is true even if the non-believer has no idea, or a false idea, of where these aspirations come from. The reason is that, just as there are not several kinds of love, neither is there more than one way of giving oneself. To give oneself to one's brothers is *always* the same as giving oneself to Jesus Christ, and, in him, to the Father.

A Christian, therefore, should fearlessly join hands with all men of good will who work for the integral and harmonious development of man and the world. He should work alongside them in every kind of undertaking, whether great or small, according to his situation and his abilities. He should join his effort to theirs, and he should encourage those who are fearful or who have never been asked to

participate. He should, under the guidance of the Holy
Spirit, make straight the ways that are adopted—for the
end does not justify the means. And he should believe with
all his strength in the presence of the Risen Christ in this
activity. He should contemplate Christ in such a way that
the men who observe the Christian see, in reality, Someone
whom they had never noticed before.

The whole theory of action, in Catholic Action, is based
on faith in the presence of Christ in any activity which is
for man's benefit. Many militants, no doubt, have gone
beyond their duty in working for their brothers without
suspecting that they were working for Christ and with
Christ. As we mentioned earlier, it is sometimes only after a
very long time that they become aware of it. Some do not
even discover it until after death, at which time they
learn the truth from Jesus himself as he told them, 'The
man to whom you gave food because he was hungry, the
man to whom you gave clothes because he was in need, the
man for whom you fought to obtain a living wage—I was
all of those men.'

When we encourage someone to work for others, and
when we join him in that work, we are actually causing him
to enter into the Mystery of Christ; we are putting him on
the road to an encounter with Jesus; we are perhaps even
making it possible for him one day to make a *conscious*
response to Love.

Some people worry about what distinguishes a Christian
from a non-Christian. If there is no difference between the
two, they reason, then there is no point in having faith. In
this respect, we must avoid two major pitfalls. The first is
to make God's love for man, and man's love for God, the
private property of duly baptised and registered Christians.
The second is not to be able to recognise what essentially

constitutes a Christian response to God's love.

God does not make distinctions between men. All, without exception, have been loved from all eternity. All have been born, and are born anew each day, in Christ. All have been taken by Christ unto himself. All have been 'carried', with their sins, their sufferings, their struggles, their whole lives, by Christ the Redeemer. All have been saved.

No man knows of anyone who is not included in Jesus' conquering love. When the Father looks at man, he 'sees' him in his Son, permeated with his love. We should look at man in the same way as God. We should consider all men with great benevolence and invincible hope; for God is in them.

All men of good will who rise above themselves for the sake of an ideal—regardless of the label which they attach to that ideal—and who forget themselves for the sake of their brothers, all such men are working with Jesus Christ and for him. They are mysteriously united to him. It is correct to say, then, that it is not absolutely necessary for a man to know Jesus Christ in order to be saved. That is, it is not necessary that he know Jesus clearly, on this earth. For a man will be judged according to his treatment of his brothers, and especially of the poorest among them, even if that man is unaware that in dealing with his brothers he is dealing with Jesus Christ himself (see *Matt.* 25:31–46).

We Christians must therefore rid ourselves once and for all of our irritation when we see that, in daily life, there is little or nothing to distinguish us from non-Christians.

We must not be shocked when, on the construction site which is the world, we see non-believers and even atheists among our fellow workers who surpass us in generosity and self-denial for the sake of our brothers. On the contrary, we should be altogether delighted. Nothing is so repellent to non-believers as that aura of self-centred superiority with which we surround ourselves either consciously or unconsciously and of which we seem unable to rid ourselves. We seem to think that we can have everything for ourselves alone—everything: truth, goodness, and even God. We think that we are rich and that we can afford to give generously to everyone else; whereas, in reality, we possess nothing. And least of all do we possess God. It is God who possesses us. It is God who loved first, and if we believe, then we must first of all believe in that love. We must believe that God loves us infinitely and personally, and that he loves all men equally, without exception and without distinction. If we can bring ourselves to accept that and believe it, our relations with non-believers will be totally different.

All men are loved. All men are saved. All men must respond to that love. And it is in that response that Christians differ from non-Christians.

God's love does not force itself upon unwilling man. Man can receive it only if he is willing. Christ cannot save us in spite of ourselves, without our help. A lover cannot demand that his love be returned. But when the loved one freely returns love, then there is a true relationship of love —that is, true love, which is simultaneously a giving and a taking. Like every lover and every friend, Jesus cannot ignore man's liberty without doing violence to human nature, without treating man as a child; without, in fact, negating his love for man.

Man, for his part, can fulfil himself only in responding with love to Jesus' love. The same thing is true also for the world; it cannot reach its full development unless man uses love at each step of its construction.

The redemptive Incarnation of Jesus Christ is perfect. Now, for man and the world to be perfect, it is necessary that they both be subordinated to man's loving response in life.

And that is the first distinction to be drawn; a distinction between those who respond to love and those who do not. And it matters little that man is required by circumstances to shout out, or to whisper, his response.

Man, of course, can say, 'No'. That possibility, which can also express itself by a definite and final rejection, is, as the Gospel points out, a great mystery. It can be understood only in the light of a love which requires the existence and exercise of complete liberty. It is, therefore, a proof of God's love, and not, as some would have it, an indication of God's indifference. God's love is never lacking to man; it is man's love that is lacking to God: . . . 'whoever comes to me I shall not turn him away; because I have come from heaven, not to do my own will, but to do the will of him who sent me. Now the will of him who sent me is that I should lose nothing of all that he has given to me, and that I should raise it up on the last day' (*John* 6:37–39).

Of all those who say 'yes' to God, only the Christian can give a conscious response with full knowledge of what is involved. The Christian *knows* that the Father has always loved. He believes it, because he has met Someone, Jesus Christ, who told him, revealed it to him. And he trusts that Someone. Jesus 'has let us know the mystery of his (God's) purpose, the hidden plan he so kindly made in Christ from the beginning . . . that he would bring everything together under Christ, as head, everything in the heavens and everything on earth' (*Eph.* 1:9–10). So the Christian knows that, when he works with his brothers for the good of the world, Jesus is there among them; and he knows that he may encounter Jesus there. He knows, too, that he is working with Christ for the execution of the Father's plan for the universe.

There are non-Christians, we have said, who say 'yes' to

God's love. Some of those who say 'yes' are even atheists. They speak their answer through their lives, and particularly through their work on mankind's behalf, although they have no idea of where the question comes from, or even of the identity of the one who asks it. They give their response through the intermediary of persons, or through loyalty to a doctrine, an ideal in which they believe. They believe in the well-being of other men, and they are determined to achieve that well-being even at the cost of their lives; but they do not know that the goal toward which they are working goes infinitely beyond earthly benefits. They want to build a just, free, and peaceful world; but they do not know that their undertaking has a supernatural, interior dimension of which they are unaware. They are like workmen who, forgetting themselves, build a solid and beautiful house, without knowing for whom, and at whose order, they build it. Jesus will judge them according to that work and its value; and its value may not be less than that of the work of those who build in full knowledge of what they are doing. But Jesus will judge them, above all, according to how much 'heart' they will have put into their work.

In this way, Jesus accepts also the 'yes' of those who come to offer it to him in a roundabout way; he accepts it even if the man who offers it, being blind, does not see the face and the hands of the one who accepts in order to give it, in turn, to his Father. For all life comes from the Father, and all must be returned to the Father.

If it is not absolutely necessary to know Jesus in order to collaborate with him, and if the work of the faithful and generous non-believer or non-Christian can have the same value as that of the Christian, then what is the point of preaching Jesus Christ? Why should we accept the 'mission' that the Father, in and with his Son, has entrusted to us?

We have no intention of straying into the theologians' field. But we cannot help stopping to reflect for a moment on this question. It is a question that comes up, sometimes painfully, among militant Christians who are working with non-believers. And it occurs, perhaps more than elsewhere, among men who have given up everything in order to go into the world and preach the Risen Christ.

The images that we have already used determine the direction of our reflections. Could we bear the blindness of our brother if it were possible for us to cure him? A blind man can walk, and sometimes he is better and faster at it than the man who can see. Guided by others, 'enlightened' by their words, he can form an image in his mind of the road to be travelled. And yet, he does not *see*. He travels through life without ever seeing the sun, without seeing the roads on which he walks, without seeing where he is going, without seeing the people around him, without ever seeing love in someone's face. His life, it is true, can be useful, and beautiful. But he is still mutilated.

In the same way, a man cannot be fully himself unless he knows who he is, whence he comes, and where he goes. An animal is a perfect animal without knowing or caring about 'why' or 'how', without being able to participate in his own development, and without being able to offer that development. It is man's prerogative, his basic dignity, to *know*, to become himself by means of himself. But for man to become himself, he must become a son of God in Jesus Christ. That is a fact that everyone should know.

If we can cure someone of his disability, then we have no right to allow him to remain disabled—particularly if his infirmity is one which affects his very being. We have no right to let a man make a mistake about his destiny, even if God, in his infinite love, and to prevent that man from suffering because of *our* wilful negligence, allows him to work, in darkness, for the creation of the world. We are responsible for that man; and we are liable for his mistakes. 'Woe to me if I do not preach Jesus Christ', cried St Paul. He did not say, 'Woe to those to whom we do not preach Jesus Christ'. Woe to *us* if we allow ourselves to violate man's dignity to the point of letting him live his life without ever hearing of that Mystery of Jesus Christ which has been revealed to us.

Once again, let us say that the best way to approach the mystery of human destiny is by way of love.

Some time ago, a woman told me how, after twenty unhappy years, she had found her missing son. The young man, hesitant and still astonished, with trembling fingers touched, caressed, and explored the face of his new-found mother. 'You are my mother!' he cried.

For twenty years he had been the son of that mother. His life had sprung from her life. But he had never seen her. He did not know her name. He had everything, in a sense, because he had life. But, in another sense, he had nothing, since he did not know the source of that life. He did not know his mother's face. His mother had never held him in her arms, and he had never been able to embrace her.

The tragedy of many 'alienated' people today, and especially of the young, is that they do not know their mothers or their fathers; they do not believe in—or they cannot believe in—their love. They are not loved, or they do not know that they are loved. And the psychologists tell us that that ignorance, or that absence, is the primary cause of social maladjustment.

There are many men who do not know their true Father in heaven, the Father who loves them more than any earthly father. They have received life from him, but they do not know either his name or his face. They do not know that they are infinitely loved by him, and that that love follows them and gives new life to them at every moment of their lives. They do not know that they are heirs to a great heritage because of Jesus Christ, and that that heritage is life itself—divine life, for today, tomorrow, and forever.

Just as we should do all that we can to help the child of an unknown father find his father—particularly if we know the father, and know him to be both loving and lovable—so too we must do all in our power to reveal God's love to our brothers. We must, in other words, act as the sons of God that we are. For we are not a father's children simply because we have received life from him without having asked for it, but also because, knowing to whom we owe life, we can accept it willingly and express our gratitude by offering the best gift that a father can receive: our joy in living from his life. Love can exist only if it is received and returned consciously.

We have a tendency to take too lightly our responsibility for the errors and ignorance of our fellow men about themselves, their life, and the life of the world. We often say to ourselves (or we act as though we had said), 'Well, after all, what does it matter whether they know where they come from and where they are going. The only thing that matters is that they are sincere, in "good faith". They've started out on the right road, and they'll get to where they are going. God will take care of that.'

That is a shocking attitude, based on perverted reasoning. It means not only that we do not love our brothers with all our hearts, as we are obliged to do, but also that we hold them in contempt and have no regard for their essential dignity.

Moreover, we forget, when we feel that way, what we have received as the People of God: the Church, the deposit of Revelation, which is the most extraordinary gift that it is possible to receive. It is a gift from God which, of all gifts, must not be hidden under a bushel basket, but must be displayed for all to see. And it is a gift of which God will demand an accounting.

God the father is always looking for his children. He revealed himself in Jesus Christ, but Jesus, although still living among men, is no longer wholly perceived as a man. Christians, therefore, as members of Christ, should individually and collectively offer their lives to God so that God may, through them, by them, and with them, be the contemporary of all modern men. Through us, Christ should be able to continue to reveal Love, and the name of Love.

If there were only one man in all the world who did not know Christ, then we would have to search the world to find him and reveal Christ to him so that that man might come to know his Father, love him, and allow the Father to love him also.

A few decades ago, we all admired militant Christians who, living in the midst of the world, were eager to bear witness to the historical Christ, to preach him openly, to shout his name from the rooftops. Fearlessly they declared their love for him, explained him to their friends, and invited everyone openly to share Christ with them. They cared not one bit whether their efforts were met with a welcome or with hostility. The Jocists[1] used to sing,

> *Let us march to victory.*
> *Let us march with pride,*
> *and nothing will stop us. . . .*

[1]The acronym for *Jeunesse Ouvrière Chrétienne* (Young Christian Workers), a very militant Catholic youth movement, active in France particularly in the forties and fifties. (*Tr.*)

Those were the days when the first priest-workers used to preach Christ in public places and hold the Way of the Cross in subway stations.

Attitudes have changed since that time. One no longer speaks Jesus' name out loud or in public. We whisper it into someone's ear so as not to disturb other people or to seem to want to force our own ideas on them. There are also innumerable rules to be followed today, sensibilities to be respected, stages to be observed, and so forth. Above all, however, it is no longer a matter so much of preaching Christ as it is of waiting for someone personally to discover his presence in others and in life. Christians must be prudent. They must not interfere; but they must be quietly present.

Every once in a while there is friction between those who believe in preaching and those who believe in silence. Both sides, either nostalgic for the past or fanatical about the present, shout abuse at each other and exchange excommunications. 'You have lost the faith', they scream. 'You understand nothing about evangelising!'

We surely do not expect Christians to climb up onto their factory benches or their filing cabinets and ask their fellow workers to observe a minute's silence at three o'clock on Good Friday afternoon. But we do not expect them to remain silent forever on the pretext that the time 'is not ripe' to speak out. And we do not expect them to neglect to preach Jesus on the pretext that true evangelisation consists essentially in living Jesus daily among men. Somewhere between the two extremes there is a middle ground on which these two attitudes can be reconciled and synthesised. And Christians should stand on that middle ground.

We must indeed preach Christ Jesus. We are obliged to do so. But we are not obliged to preach, as it were, any

Christ Jesus at any given moment and in any way possible.
We know that we must individually encounter Christ in
both of his dimensions. By the same token, it is the *total*
Christ whom we must reveal to our contemporaries—the
Jesus of Nazareth who came two thousand years ago to
save man and the world through love, and the Risen Christ
who today lives a mystery of love in human history. These
two approaches are indispensable and inseparable. They
serve to reinforce each other. To neglect one or the other
would be to mutilate Jesus and to distort his message.

We cannot deny that, in the past, we have been too often
content to preach Jesus—if not to 'teach Jesus'—without
bothering to help our brothers to *meet* Jesus, who is
present and active in their lives. How on earth could they
believe in a Jesus who died and rose from the dead if we did
not tell them about the Jesus who is alive today? And how
could they believe in the living Jesus if they did not have
the chance to meet him?

All this is perfectly true, of course. But, again, we must
be wary of going to extremes.

Earlier we asked whether there was anyone left today
who was preaching Jesus Christ. We meant someone who
speaks openly of the person of Jesus, without excuses.
Someone who declares, 'The one in whom I believe and
whom I love is not Allah. It is not the Buddha, or Marx, or
Lenin, or even Mao or Marcuse. It is Jesus Christ. I trust
him, and I try to live my whole life, my commitment, my
struggles, with him and in him. For I am convinced that
they were his struggles before they were mine.'

I have had the opportunity several times, in meetings
and gatherings of various kinds, to hear Christians openly
bear witness to their faith. They spoke openly of Jesus,
ignoring the uneasiness, the prudent advice, and the dis-
approbation of priests and laymen who thought that it was

'not the right time', that the people were 'not ready', that those who heard them 'would not understand'. On each and every occasion, their testimony was received not only respectfully and sympathetically, but even enthusiastically. The general reaction was, 'Finally, someone is talking to us about Jesus Christ.'

We are very happy and proud about all the research and all the studies that have been made on the subject of evangelisation. We are also happy and proud of the technical progress that has been made in catechetical science. But now we are tempted to say, 'Hold it. That's enough. Let's not be so concerned with perfection in the initial stages, or we'll get bogged down at the stage of pre-evangelisation, or pre-catechesis, or in the stage preparatory to pre-evangelisation or pre-catechesis, or . . . You've already made straight the way of the Holy Spirit. He now knows the road, and he can read the signposts. Let's allow him get to work. Let's admit that he is perfectly able to do what he is supposed to do. And let's expect to see him go off the road that we have prepared for him and cut new roads for himself. And then, let's get down to business and talk about Jesus. Let's talk loudly and clearly. People are tired of our hesitations and our discussions and our fears, of our defensiveness and our over-cautiousness. They are ready for us to reveal a living person to them—readier than we suspect.'

What we Christians must do is speak as apostles, as witnesses. A witness is someone who personally has *seen* what he talks about. Someone who has not *seen* almost always develops, embroiders, and sometimes, more or less consciously, pushes his lack of knowledge under the rug of technical jargon. We are often clumsy preachers and maladroit technicians simply because we have not *seen*—or because we have lost the habit of seeing. And that, of course, is why people do not listen to us. 'But they will not ask his help unless they believe in him, and they will not believe in him unless they have heard of him, and they will not hear of him unless they get a preacher, and they will never get a preacher unless one is sent' (*Rom.* 10: 14–15).

And St Paul is not talking about 'professional' preachers. Every Christian is a preacher. And every Christian is 'sent'.

Under the guidance of the Holy Spirit, we must be life's most enthusiastic pilgrims in the search for those signs of the presence of Christ which are man's just aspirations. Working with all our strength for the integral development of man and the universe, we should study, in the light of faith, all the 'values' of life and of activity which are the seeds of the Kingdom. We must expose those seeds to the sunlight of love so that they may grow and bear fruit. We must learn to see Jesus in those signs. We must listen when he speaks to us. We must join him to work for the eternal plan of his Father. Then, strengthened by our discovery, by our encounter, by our unity, we will become witnesses to our brothers that Jesus Christ, who came down on earth two thousand years ago, is still here today, mysteriously living in our lives and in theirs.

It is in being thus involved with all men—be they indifferent, unbelievers, or believers in another faith—that we will be enabled, not to 'bring God' to them (for God is already there, in their lives; and, moreover, we do not own God), but to reveal God to them. It is not enough that men of good will work for their brothers; not enough that individuals and groups be transformed by that work. They must know of that transformation. They must discover, bit by bit, that it is the result of a force that is beyond them because it is the strength of Love, of Jesus Christ.

That is why Christians must not be content with joining

Christ, in his Spirit, to work with him on behalf of mankind individually and collectively. We must go beyond even that. We must go to that faint trace of revelation that is in the heart of every man. And we can go there only by paying the strictest attention to what we see in other persons and in events. Then we will be witnesses, because we shall have *seen*. By our attitude, by a gesture, a word, a comment, we will be able to make known to our brothers that which we live deep within us: a mysterious communication with Jesus Christ in all our work for the benefit of man.

Let us not be too willing to allow Jesus to live incognito in the hearts of so many men. Possibly it is a lack of faith that makes us willing often to undertake a project in common with men of good faith, but unwilling to carry our mission through to its logical conclusion—that is, to reveal Jesus Christ. Certainly, Christ is well able to reveal himself within a man's heart. But he has chosen to make use of us in order that he may become known.

Every Christian is born in order to reveal Love and the name of Love. If we love Jesus Christ, we cannot allow him to remain hidden from the eyes of men. We must reveal him, openly and fearlessly, so that all men may live by him and in the light of his presence.

10. To Live Jesus Christ

We must encounter Jesus of Nazareth, not only to contemplate him but also to live him. And he waits for us in the Gospel, the purpose of which is to unite us to Jesus.

It is a matter of either believing or not believing that God has spoken to us. If we believe that 'At various times in the past and in various different ways, God spoke to our ancestors through the prophets; but in our own time, the last days, he has spoken to us through his Son' (*Heb.* 1:1–2); if we believe that Jesus Christ, in revealing the Father and his infinite love, expressed himself by means of a human life and in human words; if we believe that four of his Apostles, guided by the Holy Spirit, recorded the essential parts of his message for the instruction, and liturgical and missionary participation, of the first Christian communities; and if we believe, finally, that through the Gospels, in Jesus Christ, God not only spoke to the first Christians but also continues to speak to man in any era—if we believe all this and we do not regularly have recourse to the Gospel, then we are totally without understanding and we cannot call ourselves Christians. That is we cannot say that we are 'of Christ'.

It is possible that we have lost the habit of making free use of the Gospel. Perhaps we have explained the Gospel so much, written so many commentaries, studied it so scientifically, 'utilised' it so often to illustrate and explain and defend our theses, searched it so assiduously to find a formula for Christian life, and discussed it so much that we can no longer communicate with it.

I do not mean to denigrate the importance of scientific

studies of the Gospel. What we must do, however, in integrating the results of such studies into our knowledge is to keep in mind, as we read the Gospel, the rich but simple attitude of a lover who reads a letter from his beloved. For such a man, words are only an intermediary. What the eyes of his body, and even those of his mind, cannot reveal, is revealed by the eyes of the heart.

We must approach the Gospel 'religiously'; that is, with eyes other than those of our body. We must use the eyes of our minds, certainly. But we must also use the eyes of faith. In the Gospel, it is Jesus who appears before me, and speaks to me. I must communicate with his Word just as, in the Eucharist, I communicate with his Body. The Holy Spirit, who guided the Apostles when they were writing the Gospel, guides us today when we read what they wrote so that we may live from it.

I mentioned in another work the comment of a young girl who, in familiarising herself with the Gospel, had discovered the perfect way to approach the Word of Christ: 'I get up a half hour early every day to read what Jesus has to say about that day. . . . During the day, at work, I often think of what Jesus said that morning.'

Man, through love, goes freely before God, and God appears freely before him. If a man is faithful to that extraordinary meeting, he will gradually be changed—like a man who sunbathes every day. Jesus will say to him, 'I shall not call you servants any more, because a servant does not know his master's business; I call you friends, because I have made known to you everything I have learnt from my Father' (*John* 15:15).

I am convinced that Christians are too willing to give up personal contact with the Gospel. As we abandon it, we find ourselves loudly demanding from man what we did not dare ask of the Man-God. We cannot but be impressed and appalled by those millions of Chinese who are never without their little 'red book', who read it daily in order to understand the thought of their idol, and who study Mao's maxims. And let us not say that all this is carefully staged. Is it possible that Christians believe less in Christ than the Chinese do in Mao Tse-tung?

'Lord, who shall we go to? You have the message of eternal life' (*John* 6:68–69).

An artist who stands studying a painting understands more about it than does a layman. He discovers harmony, emotion and thought beneath the lines, forms and colours. Through these things, the artist goes beyond an ordinary man in his reaction.

The lover who receives a dried flower in a letter from his beloved goes far beyond the few desiccated petals. He sees 'beyond'. Through the flower, which is a symbol, and because of it, he is united to a person, a love. He communes with that love.

The Christian, too, sees things. In the face of mankind, of history, and of the world, he sees further than other men. Where other men see only the surface of beings, things, and events, the Christian perceives them as they are, in their 'inner dimension'.

If the Christian sees more deeply, it is because he has a special eye, a sort of sixth sense—which comes to him as a result of faith.

The real 'new man', whom our non-believing brothers dream of 'creating', is the Christian. The Christian is recreated in Christ. Jesus said to Nicodemus, 'I tell you most solemnly, unless a man is born from above, he cannot see the kingdom of God' (*John* 3:3); and St Paul adds, 'For anyone who is in Christ, there is a new creation' (*2 Cor.* 5:17).

We say of lovers that they are in each other's heart. Jesus has all men in his heart. In him, because of the Redemption, man has assisted at the death of non-love and of a merely human life. In him, man has been raised up: 'Whoever listens to my words, and believes in the one who sent me, has eternal life (*John* 5 :24).

The Christian is a man who, believing in Christ, is reborn in him to Love and to a 'new life'—to divine life: 'You too must consider yourselves to be dead to sin but alive for God in Christ Jesus' (*Rom*. 6:11). He has become a true child of the Father, and he must behave as such. He has the power to do so, and henceforth he can hope as the Son hopes, love as the Son loves, and see as the Son sees.

The Christian shares in Christ's prophetic gift. A prophet is not someone who predicts the future, but someone who 'sees'—that is, a man who is able to read events in the light of God. A prophet lives in the midst of life. He lives the life of his brothers. But he is able to discover the essential meaning of that life, and he announces it to his brothers who do not 'see'. And Christ, of course, is the prophet *par excellence*, for he has seen all things.

What the world needs is Christians who are prophets. And it needs many of them, and perfectly lucid ones. Men today no longer know why they are alive, and Christians have too often offered them life-styles rather than reasons for life. Prophets who 'see' in Christ will rediscover, for themselves and their brothers, the meaning of life. They will save history!

No man can become a prophet simply by wishing to be one. There are some people today who believe, and say, that they are prophets. But too often they proclaim only what they *think*, and not what they have *seen*. The true prophet is a man who, within the framework of the community of the Church, consents to die to himself in his way of 'seeing things' and to embrace God's way of seeing things. To become a prophet involves arduous and lengthy training, and a series of painful purifications.

We must learn to *see*. The spiritual value of our life depends, first of all, on how well we see, on our 'degree of vision'. Even on earth, we can develop that vision to a fantastic degree. Later, if we are loyal, we will see God face to face, 'as he really is': 'We are already the children of God but what we are to be in the future has not yet been revealed; all we know is, that when it is revealed we shall be like him because we shall see him as he really is' (1 *John* 3:2). But on earth we must learn to see the living Christ in people, in human aspirations, in activity, and in events. The whole of life must be seen and lived in the light of faith: 'The life I now live in this body I live in faith: faith in the Son of God who loved me' (*Gal.* 2:20).

Militant Christians of Catholic Action, above all, have taught us to look at our lives through the eyes of the new man. They have trained us in the confrontation of Jesus in the Gospel. They have taught us how to listen for Jesus' words through all the circumstances of our life. And they have shown us how to progress from a religious interpretation of events to an involvement in action for the sake of our brothers. The whole of this approach is called a 'review of life'. And many Christians—laymen, priests, and religious—have discovered the enormous benefits which it entails.

This 'review of life' can be badly understood and badly lived. It must not become a 'technique' for analysing situations and attitudes, or a measure of the human effectiveness of activity, or a form of intellectual gymnastics which proceeds from fixed guidelines to the dissection of an event. Even within the Catholic Action movement, there were some who did not avoid such temptations—as many people, particularly foreigners, were quick to point out. People within the movement wanted to demonstrate the 'review of life', and observers merely smiled, or reacted violently to what they regarded as a very complicated and specifically French method which, when carried to an extreme, was a distortion of the vaunted Cartesian spirit. In this case, as in others, technique overpowered mystique. Certainly, the 'review of life' is a remarkable discovery which has affected our time more than we perhaps realise. Many men have made use of it in many fields, as a peda-gogical, psychological, or sociological method. But for the Christian it is and must remain a religious approach. It is up to those movements which use it in common to see that their members do not distort it.

It is always easier to perfect the form of a religious approach than to live its spirit. Those who become dis-couraged and abandon the enterprise, however, will lose a great deal as regards the depth of their spiritual commit-ment and the authentic evangelisation of their milieux.

For our part, what we would like to do is emphasise the review of one's personal life as a spiritual approach. (We would say 'as a spiritual exercise'; but that term, through over-use, has lost much of its meaning.) I am absolutely convinced that, along with the reading of the Gospel as described above, the review of one's personal life should be at the centre of the spiritual life of a modern Christian.

We all know how difficult it is to be silent while another man is speaking. It is even harder to be silent so that we may hear God's voice. Nonetheless, every day we should stop all activity for a while and look back over the events of the day as a whole. We should pick out a particular moment, or event, of that day, and ask ourselves questions like these about it: What does Jesus want to tell me by means of that event? What does Jesus expect of me in this situation, with those persons, in those circumstances? What response will I make to Jesus?

I do not mean that we should indulge in an elaborate reasoning process, but that we should withdraw into ourselves in an attitude of simple faith: 'Jesus Christ is here, mysteriously present. I know it, because he has said that he will be with us always, even to the end of time. He is waiting for me, like a friend: "I shall not call you servants any more . . . I call you friends". With him, I can discover and realise the Father's plan of love: "My food and drink is to do the will of my Father".'

We must not be afraid of making mistakes. The Holy Spirit accompanies us and guides us in our daily pilgrimage to Christ, and we must ask him to do so. In the review of life, prayer and contemplation should play a greater part than the intellectual analysis of situations.

If we are faithful in our meetings with Christ in daily events, little by little he will enlighten us and we will see more clearly. For Christ is less hidden than we think. Our eyes are simply not accustomed to looking at him through the darkness of our senses. Jesus Christ calls us. He transforms us, and the suffering involved in that progressive purification certifies to the authenticity of our approach.

Those who, judging from externals, think that the review of life is an 'easy way' are very much mistaken. After the exhilaration of the encounter, one learns very quickly that nothing is more demanding than obedience to Christ in daily life. In order to achieve union with him, we must gradually renounce our own plans and desires and replace them with the Father's plan which is realised in Jesus Christ. Initially, the two points of view are far from conforming to one another. But, after our death-to-ourselves there is the resurrection. And anyone who is willing to risk each day of his life for Christ—whatever that life may be

—will enter into peace and joy.

Men with much experience say that 'life is the best teacher'. What they say is true; more true than they know. Jesus teaches us and transforms us in life and through life by bringing us to the concrete, historical realisation of his mystery of love. We have only to respond freely to the Saviour's daily invitation. The 'exercise' which we call the review of one's personal life can help us. It can show us how to bind together ever more tightly the spiritual and the temporal. It can teach us how to live a life, and a Christian life, transfigured by love—that is, how to be simultaneously totally present to Jesus Christ, and totally present to life.

It is a curious mistake to believe that God is silent. He speaks. But often man does not answer. Nevertheless, man needs contact with God—which is to say that he needs prayer—because he was made by God and for God. Without that contact, man undergoes a sort of progressive spiritual asphyxiation. He is like a fish out of water. He becomes a spiritual orphan, and he begins to look around for compensations. The man who does not pray, or who no longer prays (if he once knew God), looks for, or invents, something outside of himself which he can make into an idol, a god-substitute, for him to enter into contact with. The worst thing that can happen is for man to choose himself as his own idol—his body, his emotions, his ideas. Then he has only himself to talk to. He is isolated. And that is what hell is.

There is another sort of tragedy that is not uncommon in today's world. It is the tragedy of men whose inability to go out of themselves, to relate to others and to an Other, is such that it constitutes a psychological disorder. It is a 'mental illness'. And the psychologists tell us that *all* mental illnesses are the result of difficulties in relating to others. Such men, of course, are not responsible, since they are ill. Nevertheless, they are no longer men. They have lost their human nature. And that is the tragedy of it all, not only for those affected but for all mankind. For all men are responsible. We have built a society that destroys its members. We have corrupted interpersonal relations at all levels by ridiculing and debasing love. And we have neglected to connect life and man to God. Outside of this latter, essential relationship, there can be no real relationship of love between men. Without it, no society, regardless of how 'just' its structures may be, can better its members.

Unless we are very careful, we will atrophy man by cutting him off from his source. And this spiritual under-development will not be the least of the collective sins of mankind at a time when man's growing awareness and his control over the world require, rather, a spiritual over-development.

Unless we pray, and unless we pray more than did the men who preceded us, then we shall destroy ourselves.

It is not easy to pray. What seems to bother modern man about prayer is that praying is 'talking in a vacuum'. It is true that, in order to assert the transcendence of God, we have often placed him beyond and above life, in heaven. And then we asked man, when speaking to God, to detach himself from earth and to raise his eyes to heaven. Men tried to do it. And many men exhausted themselves trying. And then they gave it up, because they could not *see* the God to whom they were speaking, and because they could not hear his answer. Everything was dark and silent.

By disincarnating God we have disincarnated prayer. Here, again, we are acting as though Jesus Christ had never come. Certainly, we must pray 'Our Father, who art in heaven'; but only, so to speak, after we have met Jesus Christ. For it is Jesus who reveals the Father to us and leads us to him. It is Jesus who teaches us to speak to the Father. And outside of Christ we will never find the road to God.

No one, as Jesus said, has ever seen the Father. But men have seen Jesus Christ, touched him, heard him speak. Like them, we can meet him, listen to him, and answer him.

Jesus Christ is alive among us. He speaks. He opens the dialogue. It is up to man to answer. And to pray is above all to answer God, who speaks to man through Christ, who lives today.

God speaks to us in the Bible, and especially in the Gospel. He also speaks to us in life, in events.[1] After what we have learned about reading the Gospel and about the review of one's personal life, it is easy to understand why these approaches should determine the two dimensions of our prayer.

In one section of France, when young people start courting they are said to be 'talking to one another'. Once more, folk wisdom has gone to the heart of the matter. True love begins with mutual knowledge, and the latter can be the result of conversation. We must come to know Jesus of Nazareth by talking with him, and it is through the Gospel that we will succeed.

(I wonder why it is that when we talk about prayer, we almost immediately think about asking God for something. It is as though we want to get into God's good graces, just as we try to establish well-placed 'contacts' in the world, so that our will may be done on earth!)

Love is freely given and freely taken. It is an exchange.

---

[1] I certainly do not intend here to de-emphasise the real presence of Christ in the Eucharist. My intention here is to emphasise, for the sake of those who complain of 'Jesus' silence', that Jesus speaks to us in the Gospel and in life, and that, moreover, he waits for our answer.

Each of the lovers reveals himself to the other, and the two are thus united. After that, they can no longer refuse anything to each other. Similarly, Jesus makes himself known in the Gospel. He reveals the depths of his soul. Prayer is a response to that revelation, no more and no less. It is a conversation with Jesus, a request for explanations, an expression of admiration and gratitude. It is also an explanation of oneself by telling of one's own life and comparing it to that of Jesus.

When friends no longer speak to each other, their friendship weakens and dies. Sometimes one of them, still faithful, continues to speak to his friend, but without getting any answer. Then there is indifference, or a breaking off of relations: 'I don't talk to him any more.'

There are many Christians who don't talk to Jesus any more, even though Jesus continues to talk to them through the Gospel. This is a senseless tragedy. If we have God for a friend, we should never let that friendship die.

Jesus Christ also speaks to us through events. We've already said that, except in the case of a special vocation, the ordinary meeting place between Christ and man is life. The second dimension of prayer, therefore, is man's dialogue with Christ in life.

Hopefully, it is now clear that not only does Christ take an interest in each instant of man's life, but he also participates in it. He must gather all things to himself in love, and he can do so only to the extent that we ourselves are present in and consent to that life and himself. Jesus Christ will not take our lives if we do not give them to him. And, from that point, we should be in continual dialogue with Christ. On the one hand, we must ask him to rectify and purify our lives; and, on the other, we must offer our lives to him so that he may permeate them and live them with us. All our lives, therefore, must become a prayer. And, for

that, we must offer them in their totality. And we must also
be faithful to our meetings with Christ at particular
moments. The practice of reviewing our personal lives
offers the opportunity to do this. Beginning from the event
we choose, and scrutinising that event in the light of faith
under the guidance of the Holy Spirit, we are able to
engage in conversation with Christ.

True friends feel the need from time to time to talk
together. We too must stop occasionally and talk to Jesus.
We must make the difficult offering of a part of our time.

Soon, however, we will discover that there are problems.
We have said that, in order to hear God, we must be silent.
But often it is psychologically impossible for modern man
to be silent. Anyone who stops today for a moment of
prayer is immediately overwhelmed by the 'noise' of
daily preoccupations, of his desires, failures, thoughts, and
dreams. We must not lose heart. On the contrary, we
should be glad, for through these difficulties Jesus teaches
us what sort of prayer we must pray today.

I hope that I will be permitted to digress a moment here
to mention the great, and unexpected, success of an earlier
book of mine entitled *Prayers of Life*,[2] which has sold over
a million and a half copies the world over. I mention it not
out of vanity—which would be absurd—but to make a
point. The book is a collection of very simple prayers
drawn from life. And, for that reason, it answered a need
felt, apparently, by an enormous number of Christians.
These Christians wanted not only to present themselves to
God without subtracting themselves from life, but also
to integrate their lives totally into their prayers. The letters
I received confirmed what I suspected, that people were
torn between the deep desire to achieve that integration
and the advice they had always received to the effect that

[2]Gill and Macmillan, Dublin.

they must 'forget your worries, empty your minds', etc. This advice had been, in effect, to rid themselves of their bodies, of their human condition and vocation, and to behave like angels. Many readers were kind enough to write that they had been 'liberated' from that mentality.

Why indeed should a man be asked to leave his life at the door when he prays? The noise within us when we try to spend a moment with God is the irruption of life into our field of consciousness. When we pray, all the thoughts that come, even the most apparently irrelevant ones, are not 'distractions' designed to tear us away from God; they are invitations to put God into our lives and our lives into God. Prayer must never become a refuge into which we flee in order to escape from life. Every Christian, when he prays, is an ambassador from the whole world, and particularly of the people with whom he is associated and of the groups to which he belongs. He holds in his hands, so to speak, the record of his own life and of his brothers' lives in order to explain it to God. We should not try, therefore, to avoid 'distractions'. We should embrace them, for they are life, and offer them to God.

Naturally, it is difficult to remove from one's mind the things that are most important to us. And those things are precisely what we should offer to the Father through Jesus Christ—to ask his forgiveness, or to thank him, or to ask his help; but above all to ask that this person, this event, this particle of life not be diverted from its purpose but that it develop perfectly in Jesus Christ according to the will of the Father.

Let's not think for a moment that we are talking about a kind of prayer that consists in 'giving up', a kind of prayer that is easy because it corresponds to the taste of modern man. Prayer is never easy, for it is always an attempt to go out of oneself in the presence of God. What we must do instead of constantly struggling to suppress things is to struggle constantly to offer things.

The Christian who is faithful to prayer should not expect to be freed from life's cares and tribulations—for that would be a failure. But, little by little, his various pre-occupations will flow into a unified whole which, more and more spontaneously, will be directed toward God in Jesus Christ. The man who prays will never find any real vacuum or emptiness, nor will he find it necessary to resort to a kind of *idée fixe:* 'I am trying to *fix* my mind on God'—which is a rather dangerous psychological game.[3] In the wake of life's tumult and disorder, there will eventually come a veritable procession of all of life—of persons whom he meets, of his milieu, of the world—on pilgrimage toward God in Jesus Christ. And Christ, with the loving collaboration of free man, will 'bring everything together . . . everything in the heavens and everything on earth.'

Later, much later, after a long period of perseverance and faithfulness which constitutes a necessary and preliminary stage, certain Christians will be able to appear before God in a state of profound interior silence. That state will not be the result of a suppression, or a surrender, or a flight from life. Rather, it will be the just reward of those Christians who will have acquired the habit of leaving everything in Jesus' hands—of living all things in him as their lives unfold.

And then, like lovers who, after a day of constant sharing and communion, can spend a night in silence, without a sound, in tender companionship, these Christians, having forgotten nothing of life but having brought and given it all to Christ, will be able to give themselves—in silence.

[3]Human effort can do little to make us 'concentrate' on God. We must depend on God to captivate us to the extent that all our faculties are unified and our perception is sharpened.

Contemplation, like prayer, is not the special property of a certain category of Christians, of spiritual aristocrats. It belongs to everyone. Anyone who truly loves can achieve contemplation.

True love, as it develops, achieves a certain economy of words and gestures. When one reaches the stage where a mere look suffices, then one has reached contemplation. To contemplate God is to look at him and love him. This attitude, however, simple as it is, is the end result of a process. To try to attain silence too quickly is dangerous, for silence, although it can serve to convey a fullness of love which no word or gesture can contain, can also serve to interrupt a conversation.

Some Christians are called by God to retire, partially or wholly, from the world in order to abandon themselves to contemplation. Modern man has a great deal of difficulty in understanding that kind of vocation; for men tend to think in terms of efficiency, while love operates at the level of generosity. A man, for example, on certain nights wants the company of his wife. 'Leave your work,' he says, 'and come sit here next to me.' He wants his wife close to him, *inactive* for his sake; for the essence of love is not to *do* something for the loved one, but to *be* there for him. Thus, some lives consist almost entirely in being in the presence of God, withdrawn from all other beings. And that is the summit of love.

Contemplation is a 'gazing of the heart' in the light of faith. Every Christian, by virtue of his baptism, is able to contemplate God and to perceive his presence in life beyond sensible phenomena. We have already said that the Christian is a man who *sees*. He should make use of that ability to work toward the perfection of love. That is an obligation for the Christian; and it is an absolute necessity in the modern world. The more the world develops, the

more will it have need of contemplatives in its midst. The
more man becomes technologically oriented, the more he
has a need to become a worshipper. It is difficult, and it will
become more difficult, to recognise the 'inner dimension'
of creation as the universe passes progressively from the
hands of God into those of man.

When I walk in the city, I notice there is hardly a single
thing that man has not transformed in accordance with
God's command. I see no earth; everything is covered with
concrete. I see a few trees, rather spindly, standing
humbly alongside the buildings that tower over them. If I
look upward, I can see only a small slice of the sky. But I
see a modern city, crowned by daring architecture; I see
streets filled with men and traffic, and buildings like
beehives filled with busy people. I see factories, and I can
sense the workers taking raw material, working with it,
transforming it, making something of it by putting something of themselves into it. I see a world a-building. I see
man, the builder and the planner.

But nowhere do I see God.

It is true that God seems to be retiring, now that his
children are grown. He is leaving them the initiative, the
responsibility, and the work of construction. Some Christians are shocked. They think God is making a mistake in
trusting man.

We cannot deny that secularisation is taking place. It is
a fact. We must not, however, look at it as sociologists,
but as Christians. Man's power of creation is one of the
most beautiful proofs of God's love for his creature. If man
is taking over the universe, it is because God has willed it
to be so. Now that man is about to succeed, now that he is
beginning to live that 'temporal autonomy' that he had
so much trouble in conceiving, let us not call the realisation
of the Father's plan into question. But, by the same token,

we must keep in mind the nature of that plan. It is very easy to confuse the autonomy of the temporal and spiritual orders with the separation of the two. It has been the whole purpose of this book to show that the spiritual order is not foreign to the temporal order, that it is not 'alongside' it, but within it; distinct from it, but indissolubly bound to it by the will of God and by the ministry of the incarnate and redeeming Christ.

Many of the symbols of the past are, today, inappropriate to reveal the presence of the living God in a secularised world. We must find new signs that will be intelligible to the men of our time. Man needs such signs. And the most accurate and effective sign will be that of the Christian who is committed to and involved in the construction of the world, and who is, at the same time, sustained by contemplation in the midst of life.

He will be the living symbol, and, as we have said, the prophet, of the Mystery of Jesus Christ.

To sum up, we may say that the Mystery of Christ covers the whole of the life of man, of mankind, and of the universe—yesterday, today, and tomorrow. It is the mystery of the Creation, the Incarnation, the Redemption, and the Resurrection. It is a story, or a history, of love; and there is nothing and no one who is not a part of it.

To be a Christian is not only to believe in Jesus Christ, but also to be *of* Christ, of the total Christ; that is, to belong to Christ who today is living the mystery of his love. It is to enter consciously into that mystery, to commit ourselves, personally and collectively, as a people and a Church, to the great advantage of creation, incarnation, redemption, and resurrection which is the realisation of the Father's eternal plan. It is to work for the real development of man, mankind, and the universe.

To be thus committed is to commit one's life to and with the people who live around us, in our natural societies, in our social milieux, in our groups, structures, events, and history. It is to become inwardly involved, so that we may live the total reality of life and of what lies beyond life.

To become involved, however, one must love the world. No one can accomplish anything except by loving, and by loving passionately. God 'so loved the world that he sent his Son'. It is a look of love that is at the source of the redemptive Incarnation of Jesus Christ. It is a look of love which must be at the source of our commitment as Christians. Christians today must look at man, life, history, and the universe in the way that God looks at them.

If we love the world passionately, we will accept it as it is today, with its strengths and its weaknesses. We must not fear it, or be disappointed in it, or cry over it, but have confidence in it. Even if we can think of good reasons to be fearful, we should put those things out of our minds. We do not make a fire by stirring up ashes, but by finding the burning coal underneath and adding fuel to it. From that tiny beginning, a conflagration springs.

There is a fire at the heart of the world. Life is there, and it cannot die. That life is the life of the Risen Christ. Many men believe in God. Fewer believe in Christ. And fewer still believe in the Christ who is alive today. In order to be committed, we must indeed love the world. But we must also believe in Jesus Christ who is present in the world.

This attitude of faith is indispensable for Christians of our time. It is that attitude which enables us to understand, as we have explained, that there are not two times in life, a time when we live our human life as humans and look at God only indirectly; and a time when, on our knees, we offer to the Father our work, our leisure, our struggles, suffering, and joy. And it is that attitude which enables us also to understand that if the temporal and spiritual orders are different, they are none the less united in Jesus Christ and must be reunited by the mind, the heart, and the hands of Christians.

This attitude of faith will save modern man by giving a meaning to his life and his struggles, to man's painful upward climb, by finally freeing him from the necessity to fight or suffer or be happy for no purpose. Either our life has no meaning, goes nowhere, and is absurd in all of its parts; or else it is a unique moment in that great adventure of love which is the Mystery of Christ, and then it is sacred, and each of its moments carries within it the weight of eternity.

It is this attitude of faith, and the commitment which results from it, that will save the modern world. The Christian will no longer be absent from the world. He will not be content to stand aside and let it be built without him. He will be present, and he will join with Jesus to live, with him and in him, the demanding but exhilarating adventure of life—of that whole life which is the Christian life; that is, the life of Christ.

Man, life, and the world, daily permeated by the conquering love of Christ, taken by Christ and offered by him to the Father, will prosper. From this day, they will be transfigured. And tomorrow, they will be restored to life.

Nihil Obstat: Daniel V. Flynn, J.C.D., Censor Librorum. *Imprimatur:* Joseph P. O'Brien, S.T.D., Vicar General, Archdiocese of New York, 12 October 1970.